THE STATE OF RESISTANCE

About the editor

François Polet has a Master's degree in sociology from the University of Louvain (Belgium). He has been a Researcher at the Centre Tricontinental (Belgium) since 1998, where he edits publications and researches social movements of the South. His previous publications include *The Other Davos*, coedited with François Houtart (Zed Books, 2001).

THE STATE OF RESISTANCE

Popular Struggles in the Global South

Edited by
François Polet

Translations from French, Spanish and Portuguese by
Victoria Bawtree

Zed Books
LONDON & NEW YORK

The State of Resistance: Popular Struggles in the Global South
was first published by Zed Books Ltd, 7 Cynthia Street, London N1 9JF, UK,
and Room 400, 175 Fifth Avenue, New York, NY 10010, USA
www.zedbooks.co.uk

Copyright © Centre Tricontinental-CETRI, 2007
Translation copyright © Victoria Bawtree

The moral right of the editor and contributors has been asserted by them in
accordance with the Copyright, Designs and Patents Act, 1988

Designed and typeset in Bembo and Eurostile
by Long House Publishing Services, Cumbria, UK
Cover designed by Andrew Corbett
Printed and bound in Malta by Gutenberg Press Ltd

Distributed in the USA exclusively by Palgrave Macmillan, a division of
St Martin's Press, LLC, 175 Fifth Avenue, New York, NY 10010

A catalogue record for this book is available from the British Library
Library of Congress Cataloging-in-Publication Data is available

ISBN 978-1-84277-867-8 Hb
ISBN 978-1-84277-868-5 Pb

❖

The publishers would like to thank *Green Left Weekly*
in whose issue of 22 February 2006 a version of
Chapter 31 was originally published.

Contents

About the contributors

Femi Aborisade is a researcher, trade-union and human rights militant

Oleh George Junus Aditjondro is a professor at University Sanata Dharma, University of Yogjakarta, Indonesia

Guillermo Almeyra is a professor/researcher at the Universidad Autónomo Metropolitana, Mexico, political scientist and journalist, author of books on the Zapatistas, social protest in Argentina and the Plan Puebla Panamá

Mahaman Tidjani Alou is director of the Laboratoire d'Etudes et de Recherches sur les Dynamiques Sociales (LASDEL), Niger

Mauricio Archila is a professor at the Universidad Nacional de Colombia, researcher at the Centro de Investigación y Educación Popular (CINEP), Bogotà

Tamatoa Bambridge is a sociologist and researcher at IRIDIP (Institut de recherche interdisciplinaire sur le développement insulaire et le Pacifique), University of French Polynesia

Chantana Banpasirchote is director of International Development Studies Programme, Faculty of Political Science, Chulalongkorn University

Sarah Ben Néfissa is a researcher at the Institut de Recherche pour le Développement (IRD), France

Uchane Cheangsan is a political science graduate student at the University of Thammasat, Thailand

Yves Alexandre Chouala is a political scientist, chief researcher at the Groupe de recherches administratives, politiques et sociales (GRAPS), University of Yaoundé, Cameroon

Fatiha Dazi-Héni is a political scientist, specialist in the Middle East and researcher associated with the Centre for International Studies and Research (CERI), Paris

Antônio J. F. de Lima is a graduate student at the Universidade Federal do Rio Grande do Sul, Brazil

Demba Moussa Dembélé is director of the African Forum for Alternatives and member of the Council of the African Social Forum, Dakar

Abdel Nasser Djabi is professor of sociology at the University of Algiers

Hervé Do Alto is a political scientist and historian, based in La Paz

Jude Lal Fernando is a PhD student at the Irish School of Ecumenics, Dublin, and an adviser to fisherfolk organizations in Sri Lanka

Manolo García is founder and Political Director of the Servicios Jurídicos y Sociales (SERJUS), Guatemala City

Dai Jinhua is professor at the Institute of Research in Comparative Literature and Cultural Studies, University of Beijing

Sylvestre Kambaza is Director of the Congolese PREFED and President of the Dynamique des Sociétés Civiles du Burundi, de la République du Congo et du Rwanda pour des Actions Concertées dans la Région des Grands Lacs

Azza Khalil is a researcher at the Arab and African Research Centre, Cairo

Kamal Lahbib is executive secretary of the Forum of Alternatives, Morocco

Gülçin Erdi Lelandais is a Ph.D. student at the École des Hautes Études en Sciences Sociales, Paris

Héctor Lucena is a professor at the University of Carabobo, Venezuela

Frank Khachina Matanga is a professor at the School of Development and Strategic Studies, Maseno University, Kenya

Vinod Raina is coordinator of the All India People's Science Network

Jean-Marc Regnault is conference organizer at IRIDIP – the Institute for Interdisciplinary Research into Island and Pacific Development, at the University of French Polynesia

V. Selvam is a leader of the Malaysian Socialist Party and general council member of the Malaysian Trade Union Congress

Marcelo Kunrath Silva is professor of sociology at the Universidade Federal do Rio Grande do Sul, Brazil

Pablo Stefanoni is an economist and journalist, based in La Paz

Maristella Svampa is professor of sociology at the Universidad Nacional General Sarmiento and author of several books on the social movements in Argentina

Teresa S. Encarnacion Tadem is associate professor of political science, Director of the Third World Center, College of Social Sciences and Philosophy, University of the Philippines, Diliman

Ian Taylor is a professor of international relations at the University of St Andrews, Scotland

Michel Warschawski is a militant pacifist and director of Alternative Information, Jerusalem

Fiona White is a researcher at the Institute of Commonwealth Studies, University of London and collaborator with the Centre for Policy Studies, Johannesburg

Raúl Zibechi is a professor-researcher at the Multiversitad Franciscana de America Latina, Montevideo, as well as being a journalist and author

Acronyms and Abbreviations

4Cs	Citizens' Coalition for Constitutional Change (Kenya)
ADB	Asian Development Bank
AKP	Justice and Development Party (Turkey)
AMLO	Andrés Manuel López Obrador (Mexico)
ANC	African National Congress (South Africa)
ANGOC	Asian NGO Coalition on Agrarian Reform and Rural Development
ASAP	Agricultural Sector Alliance of the Philippines
ASF	African Social Forum
BAK	Coalition for Global Peace and Justice (Turkey)
BDP	Botswana Democratic Party
BIC	Bank for Information Center (Washington)
BPO	business process outsourcing
BTV	Botswana Television
CAFTA	Central American Free Trade Agreement
CCP	Communist Party of the Philippines
CDSCN	Democracy Coordination of Niger's Civil Society
CEDEJ	Centre d'Etudes et de Documentation Economique, Juridique et Social (Cairo)
CEI	Independent Election Commission (Congo)
CEO	chief executive officer
CFA	Cease Fire Agreement (Sri Lanka)
CGT	Confederación General del Trabajo de la República Argentina

CIEL	Center for International Environmental Law (Washington)
CINEP	Centro de Investigación y Educación Popular (La Paz)
CLOC	Coordinador de Organizaciones del Campo
CPD	Campaign for Popular Democracy (Thailand)
CREED	Citizens' Alliance in Reforms for Efficient and Equitable Development (Pakistan)
CTA	Central de Trabajadores Argentinos (Confederation of Argentinian Workers)
CTV	Confederación de Trabajadores de Venezuela
CUT	Central Unica dos Trabalhadores (Brazil)
DISK	Confederation of Revolutionary Workers' Trade Unions of Turkey
DOLE	Department of Labor and Employment (Philippines)
DSIP	Revolutionary Socialist Workers' Party of Turkey
DTI	Department of Trade and Industry (Philippines)
DTP	Peoples' Democratic Party, replacing DEHAP (Turkey)
EGAT	Electricity Generating Authority of Thailand
EPA	Economic Partnership Agreement
EU	European Union
EZLN	Zapatista Army for National Liberation
FARC	Revolutionary Armed Forces of Colombia
FDC	Freedom from Debt Coalition (Philippines)
FEF	Foundation for Economic Freedom (Philippines)
FFS	Front des Forces Socialistes (Algeria)
FIS	Front Islamique du Salut (Islamic Salvation Front), Algeria
FST	Social Forum of Turkey
FORD	Forum for the Restoration of Democracy (Kenya)
FTAA	Free Trade Area of the Americas
GANA	Gran Alianza Nacional (Guatemala)
GCC	Gulf Cooperation Council (Arab Peninsula), also CCEAG
GDP	gross domestic product
GMOs	genetically modified organisms
GSM	global social movements
GTEB	Garment and Textile Export Board (Philippines)
HIPC	highly indebted poor countries
HIV/AIDS	human immunodeficiency virus/acquired immune deficiency syndrome

IBD	Inter-American Development Bank
IER	Instance Equité et Réconciliation (Morocco)
IFIs	international financial institutions
ILO	International Labour Organization
IMF	International Monetary Fund
IRD	Institute on Religion and Democracy (Washington)
ITGLFW	International Textile, Garment and Leather Workers' Federation (Philippines)
JATAM	Anti-Mining Advocacy Network (Indonesia)
JHU	Sinhala Buddhist Political Party (Sri Lanka)
JPIC	Japanese Bank for International Cooperation
JVP	Janatha Vimukthi Peramuna (Sri Lanka)
KANU	Kenya African National Union
KESK	Confederation of Public Employees Trade Unions (Turkey)
LASCO	Labour and Civil Society Organization (Nigeria)
LTTE	Liberation Tigers of Tamil Eelam (Sri Lanka)
MAP	Moral Alliance for Peace (Kenya)
MAS	Movimiento al Socialismo (Bolivia)
MCB	Berber Cultural Movement (Algeria)
MDG	Millennium Development Goals
MERCOSUR	Mercado Común del Sur (Latin America)
MFA	Multi-Fiber Agreement
MOICAM	Indigenous and Peasant Movement of Mesoamerica
MONLAR	Movement for National Land and Agricultural Reform (Sri Lanka)
MOST	Management of Social Transformations (Unesco programme)
MST	Movimento dos Trabalhadores Rurais sem Terra (Brazil)
NAFTA	North American Free Trade Agreement
NARC	National Rainbow Coalition (Kenya)
NATO	North Atlantic Treaty Organization
NBA	Narmada Bachao Andolan (Save the Narmada Movement), India
NCCK	National Council for Churches of Kenya
NCEC	National Convention Executive Council (Kenya)
NDA	National Democratic Alliance (India)
NGO	non-governmental organization

NGO-COD	NGO Coordinating Committee on Development (Thailand)
NPA	New People's Army (Philippines)
OBCs	other backward classes
ODM	Orange Democratic Movement (Kenya)
ODP	Freedom and Solidarity Party (Turkey)
OFW	Overseas Filipino Workers
PAN	Partido de Acción Nacional (Mexico)
PER	Project for Economic Recovery (Thailand)
PF3	Poste Fixe 3 (secret jail in Rabat)
PIT-CNT	Plenario Intersindical de Trabajadores – Convención Nacional de Trabajadores (Uruguay)
PKK	Kurdistan Workers' Party
PLO	Palestine Liberation Organization
PPP	Plan Puebla Panamá
PRD	Partido de la Revolución Democratica (Mexico)
PRI	Partido Revolucionario Institucional (Mexico)
PROFNAF	Programa Nacional de Agricultura Familiar (Brazil)
PRONACO	Pro-National Conference (Nigeria)
PSM	Malaysian Socialist Party
PT	Partido dos Trabalhadores (Brazil)
RCD	Rassemblement pour la Culture et la Democratie (Algeria)
REGA	Rural Employment Guarantee Act (India)
ROPPA	Réseau des organisations de Paysans et Producteurs d'Afrique Occidentale (Network of Organizations of Peasants and Agricultural Producers of West Africa)
RTI	Right to Information Act (India)
SECC	Soweto Electricity Crisis Committee (South Africa)
SEHD	Society for Environment and Human Development (Bangladesh)
SENELEC	Société Nationale d'Electricité du Sénégal
SERJUS	Servicios Jurídicos y Sociales (Guatemala)
SPWMP	Samut Prakarn Wastewater Management Project (Thailand)
TAC	Treatment Action Campaign (South Africa)
TERRA	Towards Ecological Recovery for Regional Alliance (Thailand)
TSF	Turkish Social Forum

TRT	Thai Rak Thai (Thais Love Thais)
TUSIAD	Turkish Industrialists' and Businessmen's Association
TMMOB	Union of Chambers of Turkish Engineers and Architects
UAE	United Arab Emirates
UGTA	Union Générale des Travailleurs Algériens (General Union of Algerian Workers)
UEMOA	West African Economic and Monetary Union
UN	United Nations
UNDP	United Nations Development Programme
UNT	Union Nacional de Trabajadores (Venezuela)
UPA	United Progressive Alliance (India)
USAID	United States Agency for International Development
VAT	value-added tax
WALHI	Indonesian Environmental Forum
WB	World Bank
WSF	World Social Forum
WTO	World Trade Organization

François Polet

Introduction
The dynamism and challenges
of the social movements in the South

The aim of this collection of contributions from some 35 countries in Africa, Asia and Latin America is to provide a panorama of the social movements in the South that are fighting against social injustice and arbitrary politics. Although not comprehensive, it is, we feel, representative of the diversity of citizen resistance, in form, extent and effect. We have asked the authors, the great majority of whom come from the countries featured, to give reports that are committed, but lucid, on both the constraints and the dynamism of these social struggles.

If we are to understand the social movements in the South – the conditions in which they have emerged, their strategies and their reach – we must look at the particular socio-political, institutional and economic contexts in which they are rooted. One cannot but notice the great differences of situations: what is there in common between 'Bolivarian' Venezuela and the Gulf monarchies? It is thus difficult to make generalizations about the 'social movements of the South'. There is however one common characteristic of the countries of the South that is not without its consequences on how their civil societies evolve. They all fall within one of the two tendencies that correspond to the dominant discourse of the international community: the need for democracy on the one hand and the liberalization of markets on the other. Of course, like all tendencies, there are different versions and they combine in diverse ways from one country or region to another, and they are all the object of various forms of resistance and instrumentalization by social and institutional actors, both internal and external.

From the wave of democracy to the war on terror

Let us go back to the 1980s and 1990s. During this period there was a general trend in the countries of the South (and the East) for authoritarian regimes to move towards officially democratic systems. In less than twenty years, in a 'virtuous' tidal wave, the 'third wave of democratization' affected the three continents of the South: Latin America (Argentina, 1982; Brazil, 1984; Uruguay, 1985; etcetera); Asia (Philippines, 1986; Thailand, 1992; Indonesia, 1998; etcetera) and Africa (Benin, 1990; Mali, 1991; South Africa, 1994; etcetera). The notable exception, which has been widely commented upon, is the Arab world.[1]

This democratic contagion is not independent from changes in the international environment. The end of the Cold War and the reformulating of the hegemonic discourse around the principles of democracy and economic freedoms invited the Western powers to put their relationships in order and to withdraw or condition their support to regimes that had become unsavoury.[2] But in many countries the declining power of dictatorships was also the consequence of economic, financial and social crises that undermined one of their chief supports: the relative prosperity of part of the population.[3] And, finally, it was the growth of the democratic movements born within the civil society which was to undermine the legitimacy of the autocratic regimes by refusing arbitrary rule, by cultivating popular support for the democratic project and by organizing social mobilization that destabilized those in power.

However, several years later, the extent of this democratization wave should be relativized. As the UNDP Report for 2002 stressed, 'Of the 81 countries that have taken steps to democratize, only 47 are considered full democracies'. In Africa, particularly, a number of regimes managed the formal democratic process for external consumption (the holding of free elections, multipartyism and press freedom), but with almost total control over internal political life.[4]

Several studies have also shown the disillusion with democracy, if not an outright disbelief. This is essentially because the political opening up did not bring about the expected social progress. In fact, this period of democratization coincided with the turning point of liberal economics and the two 'lost decades' in terms of development. It is difficult to applaud successful political change on an empty stomach and while unemployment, inequalities and insecurity continue to grow all around.

This contradictory picture is still further overshadowed by the international security situation which has prevailed since 11 September 2001. The international community is now less concerned about the 'internal management' of human rights in countries that cooperate fully in the war on terror. This has contributed to changing the internal power relationships to the detriment of the groups struggling to deepen the democratic process – when, indeed, it does not actually give new legislative and juridical means to those in power to intimidate, if not 'terrorize' those who threaten the stability of their political hegemony

From structural adjustment to the war against poverty

The other global tendency that enables us to trace the evolution of the environment in which social mobilizations have been growing is that of the integration of developing countries into the world economy. The arguments of the funding agencies are well known: policies of budget austerity, privatization of public services, opening up to trade, foreign investment and capital flows should bring new dynamism to national economies that are inhibited by regulations and all sorts of social burdens. After a first, undoubtedly painful, stage of adaptation, the population as a whole will logically benefit from the stimulus to growth, the creation of new activities and jobs, cheaper goods, the extension and improvement of the quality of services in education, health, water provision, etcetera.

Today the difference between theory and reality is all too apparent. Although their effects cannot be seen independently from demographic and environmental factors and the strategies of national powers,[5] adjustment measures have indubitably contributed to increasing the informal economy and the precariousness of living conditions for whole sectors of the population. The first signs of social malaise were ignored or put down to 'archaic behaviour', in an ideological context in which most of the elites of the South converted to the principles of the market economy by either conviction or opportunism. However the extent of social destruction and the increase of social protest were to bring that optimism to a halt. The World Bank and the development experts who had orchestrated the formulation and diffusion of the 'model' have themselves been forced to review their diagnosis and to recognize that not only are the 'losers' of globalization more numerous than foreseen –

the majority in many countries – but this situation seems likely to endure.

From the mid-1990s, the debate within the community of development theorists has focused not so much on the reality of the relationship between liberalization and pauperization, but rather on the play of specific factors that explain the successive social crises. Are the macro-economic prescriptions badly conceived or is it their institutional framework that poses the problem? The dominant current of development assistance chooses the latter explanation: if the adjustment of the economies is to benefit the poorest, there must on the one hand be a better framework – and hence a reform of the institutions. On the other hand they must be accompanied by social programmes of compensation.[6]

This 'reform of the reform', as some have termed it, does not affect the core of the structural adjustment measures, but aims at making them socially and politically viable in the long term. It is accompanied by a formidable rhetorical counter-offensive: the poor are victims not so much of structural adjustment but of the incapacity of the rulers to manage the institutional environment conducive to these reforms. Hence, 'improved' reforms will be pursued in the name of the poor and with their participation.

The Poverty Reduction Strategy Papers and the Millennium Development Goals (MDG) embody this change of paradigm. Both these initiatives stress the notions of ownership by the government and the participation of civil society, as well as the importance of concentrating budgetary resources on programmes to eradicate poverty. They claim to have reconciled the donor community, particularly the World Bank, the governments and the organizations of civil society representing the poor. Is it a tactic employed by institutions losing legitimacy, or the latest example of the naïve voluntarism of the development community? Whatever it is, the international consensus against poverty has, up until now, helped to hide the unequal relationships between nations and within them, rather than softening the policies that create inequality and poverty.

Conditions for the emergence of mobilizations

It is striking how the socio-economic conditions are similar in the countries of Africa, Asia and Latin America. The following lists them, in no particular order and with no pretence of being exhaustive. The end of subsidized basic household commodities (milk, bread, oil, etcetera) and the rise in the prices of public services caused by privatization have resulted in a brutal fall in the consumption levels and well-being of urban populations. This same privatization of services and public enterprises has also brought about lay-offs that have severely affected the middle classes: from one day to another, thousands of State employees, invited to set up their own businesses (the 'socio-economic reinsertion' section of the adjustment package) have had to be re-classified in petty jobs (night watchmen, taxi drivers, etcetera) or in the informal economy. Industrial workers have not been spared: enterprises active in sectors that do not possess comparative advantages have had to adapt (through massive dismissals and outsourcing) or disappear altogether. Socio-professional categories who have resisted have been dismissed as corporatist groups, clinging to their privileges and blocking reforms – particularly those concerning the labour market – that should benefit 'the poor'.

In the countryside, the combined effects of the disappearance of public mechanisms to support the production and distribution of agricultural products, together with diminishing prices as a consequence of opening to imports, have created intolerable pressures on the small producers. Unable to sell their harvests at reasonable prices, they have been forced to sell their land to reimburse their debts and to seek work on the large estates or in the duty-free zones (like the *maquiladores*) – when, indeed, despair does not drive them to the most terrible way of escape: suicide.[7]

Rural communities are also regularly despoiled through the huge infrastructure projects (dams, highways, airports, oil pipelines) for the industrial exploitation of raw materials (deforestation, mines, oil), as well as the establishment of multinational corporations, tourist attractions and the urban expansion that are inseparable from 'modern' economic development. They suffer most of the negative consequences (expulsion, pollution, destruction of natural resources), without participating in the benefits.

All this deterioration in living conditions has created resistance among a broad spectrum of those concerned. But, contrary to an overly mechanistic view of social relationships, passing to open contestation of official policies is not automatic. The daily struggle for survival, which is immediate, does not get people to join social struggles for material benefits that can seem unpredictable and far-off. The observation made by Yves Chouala concerning Cameroon can very well be applied to other countries: 'This orientation of helping people to help themselves is considerably diminishing the political conscience and capacity of Cameroonian civil society, which is in complete antithesis to taking a critical approach and questioning the leadership'.

As well as material pressures there is a socio-political context that is very hierarchical: the political culture of subordination prevails in many regions. Without falling into cultural determinism, it is important to take into account the traditional weight of fear and respect *vis-à-vis* public authority, particularly in a country where the political opening up is the result not of a broad citizens' movement but of a democratization strategy planned from above. The 'owners' and the 'big men' usually remain at the centre of local political life: they are the ones who dispense protection and favours, and influence the voting and people's political behaviour.[8] Contestatory action often involves creating tensions with the clan or family network of solidarity and all the allegiances that form part of it.

However this view should also be balanced. Even in the most authoritarian contexts, when channels for representation and the expression of interests are limited or strictly controlled, a whole range of popular protest can escape the political and policing actions of their leaders. Such protests are usually different from those of the social movement in the West, often erupting into unforeseeable and uncontrollable violence. Examples are the 'bread riots' in Tunis in 1978, the 'high cost of living riots' in Morocco in 1984, or the '*Caracazo*' in the Venezuelan capital in 1989. Or they may take the opposite form, of daily 'infra-political' resistance: various kinds of encroachment, illegal electricity hook-ups, boycotts, vandalism and so forth.

There has to be a minimum confidence in the ability of the democratic system to integrate the social demands being expressed by the population before launching a collective action to make demands. Such minimum confidence is increasingly lacking in certain countries. Many have the impression that nothing has changed, or that 'all has changed so that nothing will change'. Democracy is but the new framework within which the same people will battle for power, blocking all possibilities for economic and social change. This 'democratic disillusion', which borders on cynicism when the lifestyle of leaders is contrasted with the increase in the precariousness of existence for many, leads to the boycotting of elections, a falling back into private life, prioritizing individual strategies of social promotion, emigration or integration into the networks and parties that enable people to get a share of the cake.

In these difficult circumstances, politicization work, consisting of making the connection between individual and collective experiences and the decisions taken in the political field, and the organization of the most vulnerable categories of the population, is long and tortuous. Action by the militants, veritable 'mobilization entrepreneurs', is thus decisive for a structured contestation to emerge from social dissatisfaction.[9]

Strategies and political effectiveness

What strategies are used by the social movements to influence events and to soften policies that exacerbate their living conditions? They can only be understood when seen in the context of the great inequality of relationships within the country – groups penalized by development policies are often marginalized politically, in the sense that their views and interests are not well represented in decision-making bodies (parliaments, governments) – as well as the inequality of relationships between the countries and the foreign institutions (international organizations, countries in the North, and transnationals) which influence the orientation of national policies.

These strategies depend on many factors such as perceptions by social actors of the political conjuncture and power relationships, the resources that they have at their disposal, the way in which militancy is structured, and the strategies of those in power to channel or neutralize the demands of the population. The political effectiveness of the social movements particularly depends on their ability to respond to two challenges: that of convergence between the social actors and the relationship between civil society and political society.

The challenge of convergences

One of the strategic choices that is the most logical and the most profitable for groups who are mobilized is to combine their strengths and voices with the movements that, in the region or in the country, are fighting battles close to or similar to their own. In this way the contestation broadens, becomes more visible and has greater political resonance. Necessary as they may seem, these convergences do not come about naturally. First of all, they require that the people involved stand back from their own situation, pressing as it might be, to realize what they might have in common with other groups.

This 'growth in general awareness' usually takes place through the symbolic construction of a 'framework' of a common identity or adversary. The creation of the Assembly of the Poor in Thailand illustrates this kind of strategic evolution. As explained by Vanida Tantivithapitak, one of the activists:

> The idea to unify existing issue-based networks into the Assembly of the Poor was to achieve full capacity to solve all our problems. To do so, it was necessary to think about a common movement symbol in order to unite all issue-based networks and also to solicit support and sympathy from the general public. With the concept of the poor, they would be able to explain our reasons why we were impoverished by pointing our fingers to the state and corporate projects. In this way our constant struggles and protest rallies can be understood and gain legitimacy. (Prasartset 2004)

It sometimes happens, too, that this coming together of social actors is made extremely difficult, if not impossible, by the ideological and partisan divisions that fragment the militants and the rivalries between the organizations that result from them. This break-up among the militant forces is particularly noticeable in the case of the movements of the unemployed (*piqueteros*) in Argentina and the mass movements in India. While they will normally march side by side against a common adversary, partisan logic or doctrinal rigour often overcomes the desire for collective action. Conversely, the Kifaya movement in Egypt, which brought together Nasserites, liberals, Marxists and Muslim Brothers in public demonstrations against the Moubarak regime, was the constructive and stimulating result of a long process of overcoming traditional divisions, which was made possible by the common rejection of arbitrary politics.

The challenge of convergences also involves the building of bridges between movements in different countries. The internationalization of struggles and the emergence of the global justice movement are the logical consequence of growing numbers of social actors becoming aware that an increasing number of policies that affect their local ways of living are the result of decisions taken outside the national context, within international institutions such as the World Bank, the International Monetary Fund and the World Trade Organization. And, besides the impressive development of world social forums, social opposition has emerged and is gradually being organized, although unequally, at the regional level. While continental convergences against the Free Trade Agreement of the Americas have, understandably, hit the headlines, attention should also be paid to the Asian networks against the activities of the Asian Development Bank and all the meetings between African social movements on issues such as the debt and free trade agreements.

This cross-border convergence has also come up against obstacles, as can be seen from various, quite different phenomena such as nationalist feelings which regularly upset certain civil societies,[10] the discrepancy between the 'economic' agenda of the antiglobalization movement and the 'political' agenda of the Arab democratic organizations, or the lack of representativity in the participation at the different international social forums.

The challenge of the relationship with politics

Another aspect determining the dynamics of social mobilization is the type of relationships that social movements have with actors in the institutional political sphere. For most of the social actors in the struggle it is a question of allying with individuals and parties who can directly or indirectly influence decision making that is favourable to them. In her chapter on the Philippines, Teresa Tadem cites the example of the peasants in the vegetable industry in Benguet province, who formed an alliance with the local elected authorities to prevent the central government from liberalizing the market in order to prevent their jobs from being swept away by the importation of cheap vegetables.

Such an action, which is delicate in any democratic system, is all the more so in States that have been historically 'imported' or 'imposed' from outside and where parties are not so much organizations representing interests or ideological options as electoral machines overtly created by factions of the oligarchy that are disputing power between themselves. The challenge to militants is therefore to find trustworthy support in a sphere where the superficiality of the programmes is competing with the lack of transparency in decision making, trying to prevent the social forces they are representing from being diverted or instrumentalized.

We must rid ourselves of a certain idealization of the 'popular': politicians are not the only ones to see the organized grassroots as masses for use in electoral manoeuvring. The leaders or whole organizations that succumb to the clientelism and bargaining that are part of the political sphere are not rare. An example is the way the elite of Congolese civil society profited from their participation in the inter-Congolese dialogue to assign themselves comfortable positions in public institutions. These tendencies are all the stronger in regions where 'political entrepreneurs' consider their capitalization on popular dissatisfaction as a 'primitive political accumulation', a first indispensable step in building up the social capital that will give them access to politics.

In countries where they exist, the left-wing parties are the 'natural' political allies of the social movements with whom they share, at least in words, their ideas and claims. Some of them, like the Partido dos Trabalhadores (Workers' Party) in Brazil, are historically the result, the political prolongation, of broad popular movements. The strategies adopted by these convergences vary from one national situation to another and are generally conditioned by the parties' chances of gaining access to power. They range from the dynamism of struggle and de-stabilization of institutions – as with the Movimiento al Socialismo (MAS) in Bolivia – to efforts to channel social energy in order to maintain the governability of the country. This was, according to Raúl Zibechi, the function of the referendums of 2003 (against the privatization of the State oil company) and 2004 (against the privatization of water) organized by the trade unions and the Frente Amplio in Uruguay.

The ambiguity of the relationships between the social and the political left inevitably increases with the arrival of left-wing governments to power, as can be seen in present Latin American politics. The gap, more or less great and always present, between the 'historic' project of the left and the policies carried out by governments inevitably involves greater tensions between the different parts, social and political, of the left.[11] This phenomenon is not only at work in countries where the governments have openly opted for a moderate line, like Brazil and Uruguay. In Bolivia, the MAS of Evo Morales, considered by the mass of peasant and indigenous militants as a 'political instrument' rather than a party, had to confront social opposition from the left, composed of district associations and radical trade unions, as soon as it rose to power.

These tensions sometimes lead to dramatic rifts and the formation of new militant groups who try to mobilize those affected or disappointed by the *realpolitik* of the centre-left governments. Examples include the formation of a new trade-union organization, Conlutas, in Brazil, breaking with the Workers' Party and the Central Unica dos Trabalhadores (CUT) after the pension reform of the Lula government, as well as the 'Other Campaign' led by the Zapatista Marcos, to the left of the Partido de la Revolución Democratica (PRD) of Manuel López Obrador in Mexico, or all the new social movements that are 'anti-ANC' following the privatization policies of South Africa's great African National Congress party.

Is the emphasis being put by funding agencies over the last few years on the participation of civil society in working out development strategies and the struggle against poverty a prelude to greater awareness by decision-makers of the problems raised by the movements of development victims? Perhaps, but the potentiality of these participatory arrangements depends largely on the degree of organization of civil society and the political will of those who govern. Experiences in Africa show that the new spaces for 'consultation' are mainly open to organizations that have a high profile and financial means, and that share the language and vision of international development assistance. They result in marginalization of the social actors who are more critical of the dominant policies; they also lead to the artificial building up of an obedient civil society, which gets its legitimacy from its role as intermediary between the population and the funding agencies, while giving greater legitimacy to those in government and to development experts.

The impact of resistance

The extent of the emergence and multiplication of social movements opposed to neoliberal policies is of course very different from one country or region to another, according to the intensity of the mobilization, the political context, the room for manoeuvre of governments and … the evaluation of the observers.

It is difficult to avoid citing, first of all, the development of the socio-political scene in Latin America, where the 'pink wave' of the left-wing and centre-left governments – Venezuela, Argentina, Brazil, Uruguay, Bolivia, Chile, Nicaragua and Ecuador – and the putting on ice of the Free Trade Agreement of the Americas (FTAA) are the direct result of the scale and persistence of the social mobilizations. In terms of a change in economic and social policy, the balance sheet of the Latin left-wing governments is, however, uneven. There is indeed a difference between the government of Evo Morales (Bolivia), engaged in an in-depth transformation of institutional, economic and social structures that benefits the poor and the indigenous people, as well as making possible greater sovereignty, and the government of Lula, who is trying to extend social programmes for the poorest but without rejecting the economic orthodoxy of his predecessors.[12]

The importance of the developments in Latin America should not encourage us to minimize the actions of social movements in other regions of the South. In political situations that are generally unfavourable, the first contribution of these social movements has been to help the social groups, who are paying heavily from the insertion of the national economy into the world market, to emerge from the shadows and take a front place on the political scene. Their presence and their dynamism have forced those responsible to explain their options regarding economic policies, to take into account the social consequences on the different groups of the population and to defend their interests more vigorously in international circles. Consider, for example, the more combative attitude of the leaders of West Africa within the World Trade Organization (WTO) on the cotton question. This was largely due to the pressures of the national organizations of producers on their governments and the international campaign organized by the Network of Peasant Organizations and Agricultural Producers of West Africa (ROPPA) with the support of European NGOs.

There is no doubt that popular resistance has rendered more complicated the implementation of the anti-social reforms preached by the international financial institutions. To the great displeasure of their theoreticians, many of these reforms have been halted, postponed, distorted, even simply withdrawn, following the great mobilizations that they have provoked. And there have been many local victories against projects intended to enable transnational groups to exploit natural resources as well as local victories against the large infrastructure projects that have not respected the local people. At the national level, well-publicized campaigns have enabled the rights of people to triumph over the rights of business. The Treatment Action Campaign (TAC) in South Africa, which promotes the generalization of access to generic anti-retroviral medicines – against the patent policy of the pharmaceutical multinationals, together with the inertia of the South African government – is symptomatic of these collective actions that have been effectively and intelligently orchestrated.

While these political and juridical victories are encouraging, their follow-up generally remains vulnerable and often continues to depend on the development of the power relationships within a country and between countries. Vinod Raina himself, who only two years ago welcomed the adoption, by the centre-left Indian coalition the United Progressive Alliance, of a series of laws demanded by the social movements (such as the one guaranteeing rural employment) now reflects bitterly that they have been emptied of substance by the neoliberals who dominate the coalition. Where the representativity of institutions remains problematic, the longevity of social and democratic gains in politics therefore depends on the ability of social movements to maintain a minimal degree of mobilization over a long period of time.

Notes

1   While democracy is constantly being postponed by the authorities in Arab countries, it is interesting to note the remark of Sarah Ben Nefissa (see Chapter 10) that the reactivation of civil society in the region 'is mainly based on a general consensus of the activists and civil organizations on the priority of democracy and the need for an in-depth reform in all their regimes'.

2   In 1990, in a speech at La Baule, François Mitterrand declared that from now on 'All the effort of contribution of France will be linked to the efforts being made towards achieving greater democracy'.

3   Paradoxically, structural adjustment and financial liberalization have sometimes contributed, through their disastrous social effects, to precipitating the fall of dictatorships. For example, in Indonesia, Suharto, after thirty years of solitary power, was swept away by the social and political crisis created by the financial crisis that affected his country.

4   *Almost total*, because, as Zekeria Ould Ahmed Salem has shown for Mauritania, and contrary to the linear vision of 'transition experts' about the failure or

success of the processes to democratic transition, the interjection of the democratic problematic always changes the pattern of political relationships and opens up unprecedented spaces for social actors to negotiate with the leaders (1999, p. 132).

5   Like many Africanists, Gauthier de Villers stresses the enormous ability of local powers to interpret and subvert measures which are imposed upon them from outside: 'The African authorities, in their predicament, have no choice but to accept the structural adjustment programmes and they have neither the power, the ability nor the motivation to make them soften policies, by adapting them to the realities of the country: policies that the World Bank and the International Monetary Fund tend to produce, according to a universal mould. But, being charged with executing them, they have the means of deforming the logic of adjustment by seeing that the stabilization measures spare no one except … themselves.' (de Villers 2003, p. 43).

6   Thus, for a start, the actions of the administration of a developing country must be guided by the norms of good governance: it must become more efficient, adopting the methods of the private sector; be more transparent and responsible by opening up to the participation of civil society; and guarantee private investors a juridical, social and political climate that is stable and reassuring. Then, governments must set up social programmes that are targeted and temporary to relieve the categories of the population most affected by economic adjustment.

7   As Vinod Raina says in Chapter 27 on India, the Ministry of Food and Agriculture announced in July 2006 that 100,428 peasants had killed themselves since liberalization got under way in 1993.

8   In many countries the relationship to the State is not experienced as one of rights or equality before the law but follows a clientelistic and patrimonial logic: one's network, clan or family has to get privileged access to the resources of the State.

9   It has been observed, however, that this militant vocation is increasingly rare. Many of the generation that took the leadership of the democratic movements in the 1980s and 1990s have been integrated into the State apparatus (through the ANC in South Africa and the PT in Brazil, for example). The younger ones find it difficult to resist the advantages – an air-conditioned office and First World level of salary – that are offered by a career with the NGOs or with international development organizations.

10 These nationalist reflexes are particularly sensitive in a country like Turkey (see Chapter 16 by Gülçin Erdi Lelandais), but they also occur in countries where they would be less expected, like the recent quarrel between Argentina and Uruguay about the construction of two industrial paper factories on the banks of the river separating the two countries. A large part of Argentinian and Uruguayan civil society allowed themselves to be overcome by the nationalist rhetoric of their respective governments (see Chapter 6 by Maristella Svampa).

11 On the differences between the left-wing Latin American situations, see 'Mouvements et pouvoirs de gauche en Amérique latine', *Alternatives Sud*;

Vol. XII, 2005, 2.

12 The Brazilian militants, particularly, have had the bitter experience that 'occupying the government does not mean having the power'. But the existence or not of margins for political manoeuvre (within national parliaments and local governments) as well as for economic manoeuvre (the degree of indebtedness of the country and its dependence on international markets), while they have their importance, is not the only explanation for the strategies adopted by the progressive governments. Some of the decisions taken, or not taken, by those in charge are also explained by the fact that the search for power, and then the desire to maintain it, greatly alter the internal dynamic of these parties (political calculations and concessions of all kinds often take precedence over the desire for transformation). And the historic ties with the popular movement weaken the more that the parties' electoral base and the range of their alliances is broadened.

I Latin America

Raúl Zibechi

1
From Cancún to Mar del Plata:
A continent in effervescence

The struggle against the Free Trade Area of the Americas (FTAA) has been the main motive of convergence for the social movements of the continent. From the Fifth WTO Ministerial Conference in Cancún (Mexico) in September 2003 to the Fourth Summit of the Americas in Mar del Plata (Argentina) in November 2005, the movements grew in unity of action, succeeding in creating an important space for themselves in society and the media, even getting on the agenda of the powerful.

As happened at Cancún, when a wide network of social movements caused the collapse of the conference, at Mar del Plata they succeeded in halting progress on the FTAA. On both occasions the grassroots movements, but also many NGOs, together with the progressive governments in the region, empowered the social protest – but this also imposed limits.

A list of the most important meetings and forums held in 2004 alone (see the box on p. 20) gives an idea of the vigour and range of the convergences on the Latin American continent. These international get-togethers were evolving over a decade but the frequency of the meetings has continued to increase over the last few years. The whole movement culminated at Mar del Plata, where the struggle against the FTAA, which was the objective of a large number of the campaigns and coordinated actions, ended in a resounding victory.

The role played by the indigenous and peasant movements was fundamental. The former started to organize themselves at a continental

19

2004, year of the convergences – a brief chronology

Between Cancún and Mar del Plata, almost a dozen coordination meetings of the social movements took place in 2004 in Latin America, as well as meetings at events in other regions of the world in which members of their social movements were participating. The most important of these was the World Social Forum held in Mumbai (India), 16–24 January 2004. In March, a meeting against free trade agreements was held in Mexico, organized by the Indigenous and Peasant Movement of Mesoamerica (MOICAM), which called for strengthening convergences against the Puebla-Panama Plan, CAFTA (Central American Free Trade Agreement) and the FTAA. From 19 to 21 July the Mesoamerican Peoples' Forum was held in San Salvador, which also decided to become involved in the struggle against the free trade agreements in general and the FTAA in particular.

At the end of July, the Second Continental Summit of the Indigenous Nationalities and Peoples of Abya Yala took place in Quito, which was followed by the First Social Forum of the Americas. Other convergences took place in parallel sessions: the Continental Campaign against the FTAA, the Assembly of Social Movements and the Meeting of Social Scientists of the Americas. On this occasion the CLOC (Coordinador de Organizaciones del Campo) called for a day of mobilization against the FTAA on 12 October. Early in October the Third Bolivian Encounter against Free Trade Agreements and the FTAA took place in La Paz, with the participation of the campaigns against free trade agreements of Colombia, Ecuador, Peru and Bolivia. That same month there was a meeting in São Paulo (Brazil) to discuss economic negotiations between the European Union and Latin America. In November the Chilean Social Forum was held in Santiago, attracting the largest mobilization of people since the end of the military dictatorship. In December there was the World Encounter of Intellectuals and Artists 'In Defence of Humanity', promoted by the government of Hugo Chávez. And in January 2005 the WSF met again in Porto Alegre, with the participation of over 200,000 people.

level at the time of the Continental Campaign for 500 Years of Resistance, which preceded and prepared the counter-demonstrations of 1992 against the celebrations of the anniversary of the 'discovery' of the Americas. The peasant movements have large regional coordinations, like the CLOC (Latin American coordination of organizations in the field) and Via Campesina. While the epicentre of the former is the

Andean region, the latter look to Brazil and the Landless Rural Workers' Movement. These two types of movement form the collective subjects who are most conscious of the destruction caused by free trade and it is they who succeeded in putting forward the most credible alternative to the neoliberal model.

The Peoples' Summit at Mar del Plata revealed the gains of the social movements, as well as the new problems they were confronting. It showed that there was a growing awareness of the problems created by the free trade agreements, particularly for agricultural production and the small and medium rural producers. The most recent gain, though one that has been in preparation since the 1990s, is the capacity to organize international and continental campaigns, in which the social forums have played a decisive role, alongside the coordination between peasants, indigenous people and trade unions.

However, at Mar del Plata there were evident signs of new challenges for the movements at a time when there are progressive and left-wing governments in the main Latin American countries. It was indeed the social movement that launched the challenge to halt the FTAA. In 1997, when not a single government in Latin America was hostile to the Washington Consensus, a forum of peasant, trade-union, indigenous and ecologist organizations met in Belo Horizonte and proposed the creation of a broad and diverse social alliance against the integration being dictated by the United States. The first Peoples' Summit took place in Santiago in 1998 and the second in Quebec in 2001. It was this continental campaign against the FTAA that created the conditions for defeating the project for US integration. However, at Mar del Plata it seemed that the activism (*protagonismo*) was produced by the governments while it was actually a result of actions by the social movements.

As at the World Social Forum in Caracas in January 2006, there tends to be some confusion between governments and movements. It was the latter that, through their struggles, managed to isolate and delegitimize the plans of the imperialists, but now it is the governments who are taking the initiative and attributing successes to themselves. There is no easy solution to the contradiction. It is up to the movements to work out how to operate under governments that very often take over the banners brandished by the social movements but which then act 'from above', reproducing the models of the traditional political culture. There is an urgent need to have a strategic debate, not to reject the viewpoints that are genuinely shared with such governments, but to affirm the necessary autonomy of the movements. As recent history has shown, only the social movements can guarantee the depth and sustainability of the changes to be made.

Marcelo Kunrath Silva and Antônio J.F. de Lima

2

Dilemmas for social actors
in Brazil

Understanding the dilemmas and prospects of Brazilian social and political actors engaged in struggles against neoliberalism and the subordination of social life to the interests of capital requires an understanding of these actors and struggles in the context of the historical development of Brazilian society.

Up until almost the end of the nineteenth century (1888), Brazil was still officially a society based on slavery, with a high concentration of land ownership and no clear distinction between the public and the private. Thus the country's structures and political culture were marked by hierarchical principles that excluded the vast majority of its population: poor workers from the rural and urban areas of the country (where almost all the black population were to be found). It was only in the 1930s that this situation began to change, at least partly, through a process of subordinate and selective integration of the dominated classes into the world of citizenship (which has been defined as 'adjusted' or 'permitted' citizenship).

The years from the second half of the 1970s and through the 1980s saw significant changes in these deeply hierarchical and authoritarian patterns. Rooted for the most part in the progressive Catholic discourse of liberation theology, social movements and organizations introduced – unprecedented in the country's history – a new 'subject' into the political scene: the so-called 'popular classes' (poor workers, those living in the urban peripheries, peasants expelled from their land, among others). Breaking with the 'subordinated integration' of the populist periods (1945–64) and the military dictatorship (1964–85), for the first time there were discussions and organizational forms that succeeded in obtaining the support and mobilizing part of the poorest and least educated people in Brazilian society, who had always resisted the efforts of the traditional left-wing political parties to mobilize them. Through this process, 'politics' (which had historically been understood as reserved for the elites and from which little was to be expected) made changes possible that were desired by the poorest people.

Thus, this period saw a strong 'cycle of protests', starting with a growing mobilization outside the institutional channels permitted by the military dictatorship but which gradually, to the extent that they were making democratic conquests, began contesting inside institutional politics. This movement can clearly be seen in the evolution of the Workers' Party (Partido dos Trabalhadores – PT) which, besides being a result of the process, is also one of its main agents.

Brazilian politics were distinguished in the 1980s and 1990s by the intensity of this cycle of protests and the vitality of its actors. While many of the leading countries were undergoing the dismantling of the welfare state based on neoliberal ideas, in Brazil a broad array of social and political forces were trying, for the first time in history, to build an effective State that recognized, universalized and guaranteed rights. This process brought about the formulation of a new national constitution, called the Citizens' Constitution, in 1988.

These efforts were, however, taking place in a somewhat unfavourable international context, when capitalism was being systematically restructured (creating serious social costs) and when public finances were in a critical situation through external and internal indebtedness.

Thus the situation was ambiguous, which affected the political disputes and social struggles in the country from 1990 to the beginning of the new century. Many of the social and political actors that emerged during the cycle of protests gambled on the possibility that they might be able to influence the orientation of the democracy being created in Brazil – that is, making changes for a more egalitarian and democratic society – through institutional spaces, either the traditional mechanisms of representative democracy (elections, parliaments, executives, political parties) or the new channels of social participation and representation (councils for social policies, management committees on governmental programmes, participatory budgets, etcetera) set up in the

1990s. For them, the victory of Lula in 2002 was the culmination of a process that had been going on for nearly thirty years. During this period new actors entered the political scene and there was a relative democratization in the relationship between State and civil society, as well as governmental policies and programmes to meet the demands of the poorest. In sum, there was a relative halt to the neoliberal strategies for the dismantling of the State and of peoples' rights.[1]

However this gamble (*aposta*) on the institutional channels and more particularly on the election of Lula had, by 2006, become relatively dicey. The reasons for this frustration can be attributed to three different types of diagnosis. One was identification of the burdensome structural constraints confronted by national governments, especially in peripheral countries. Another was recognition of the dominating structures and their enormous resistance and capacity to act, typical of Brazilian society: combined they represent a considerable force against progressive social and political actors, as well as being an important source for their co-optation and corruption. Finally, there was a vagueness in the new government's programme and a lack of will or ability to take advantage of the opportunities provided by the election victory by taking more radical initiatives *vis-à-vis* the dominating elites and their interests (particularly as concerns economic policies, which continue to follow the same 'stabilization model' adopted by the government of Fernando Henrique Cardoso).

Without entering into the merits of each of these diagnoses, an evident frustration has resulted, which has had a significant impact on the progressive forces of Brazilian society. Lack of a clear political line orienting the actions of the Lula government, which is formed by a coalition of parties with little in common in terms of programmes (with supporters, in some cases, who are clearly opportunistic and 'physiological'), corresponded, in its ambiguity, to the positions of the social organizations and movements who contributed to Lula's victory. During the first two years of his presidency, the social movements did not exert excessive pressure on the government, giving it time to create the conditions necessary for the expected social changes. However, already by 2005, the movements were concluding that the Lula government, because of its complex composition, was unable to make progress at the rate that they demanded. So public pressures became increasingly forceful, as illustrated by the so-called Red April convened by Via

Campesina, in 2005 and the National March of the Movimento sem Terra (the Landless Rural Workers' Movement), in which thousands of militants marched over 200 kilometres to Brasilia and made daily criticisms in the media of the federal government.

The ambiguous relationships between the movements, even those most critical, and the Lula government was once again evident when there were accusations of corruption against members of the government. Here the movements took up a dubious position: condemning the corrupt, but supporting the government against what was interpreted as an attack by the right wing to bring down (or at least to weaken) Lula before the 2006 elections.

The present period can, to some extent, be seen as the peak and also the end of that cycle of protests that started in the redemocratization process, of which the PT was the main expression and agent. As a result, there is increasing discussion about the possibilities and limits of bringing about change through the institutional political actors and spaces. In other words, there is now a debate, which was quite common at the beginning of the 1980s (and partially sidelined by the 'gamble' on institutional participation), on the need to complement or, according to a more radical perspective, replace institutional action for more combative and extra-institutional forms of political intervention.[2]

So, while there is a broad front of social actors concentrating their efforts mainly to intervene in the institutional spaces, there is a growing presence and visibility of actors, such as the Movimento sem Terra, the Via Campesina, the Movement of Unemployed Workers, the Movement of the Struggle for Housing and the National Coordination of Struggles, among others, who are oriented towards direct action or confrontation, either with the State or with other social and economic actors. There are also efforts to increase the linkages between actors, such as expressed in the Consulta Popular, with the aim of overcoming isolated struggles, as well as attempts to propose the construction of a new political project that would succeed in unifying the Brazilian popular movements.

Another development arising from this frustration is less visible, but has a strong political impact: the discrediting of and scepticism towards the political institutions, actors and projects that historically marked the attitudes of the population, especially the poorest, are again increasing. As we stressed earlier, 'politics' was, for these people, a term that was always negative, as its institutions were rejected, considered unsuitable for participation. At a particular moment, between the 1970s and 1980s, some of the structures of domination were broken and a small proportion of the population entered the political scene with relative autonomy. Then there was the long march of two decades of intense social and institutional struggle, but with meagre results in terms of effective change in the life of millions of poor Brazilians. It ended with many of these 'new subjects' leaving the scene, having to concentrate on the tough battle for daily survival.

Thus today political frustration, together with the negative effects of an excluding market and growing criminality, has caused significant sectors of society to find themselves in an almost Hobbesian situation of 'war of everyone against everyone'. Because of the lack of organized forms for the construction and expression of social and political conflicts that recognize and legitimize the vast majority of the population, inter-personal violence is increasingly spreading in everyday life.

What will the social organizations and movements and the political parties that still favour an anti-systemic orientation do? This largely depends on their capacity to become effective instruments of the expression – in the framework of political institutions and social struggles – of that part of society that has traditionally been condemned to silence and, as a consequence, reacts with the 'noise' of an increasingly intense violence. It will be a tremendous task to channel this conflict, to give it a political expression, to confront the structures of inbuilt domination and inequality and, especially, to build alternatives that can be perceived as viable. It is, however, very difficult for the social and political actors whose discourses and practices have little meaning for those to whom they are addressed. Their material and financial resources are limited and they are subjected to physical and symbolic violence. Above all there is a generalized disbelief in the power of collective action to bring about change. For all these reasons the social and political actors are not very capable of reaching and mobilizing the great majority of the poorest Brazilians.

Notes

1. This process continued even during the two mandates of President Henrique Cardoso, between 1995 and 2001, which have often been termed neoliberal but ambiguously, as a result of pressures from the movements and organizations of civil society and left-wing political forces. There were in fact victories, or the maintenance of governmental actions that could hardly fit into classical neoliberal thinking (like the National Programme for Family Agriculture – PRONAF, the programmes for AIDS support and prevention, certain programmes to guarantee a minimum income, among others).

2. This view does not, however, mean abandoning, or a simple rejection of, institutional intervention. In spite of the critical conjuncture, the PT still has considerable presence among social organizations and movements, and it remains the main instrument for the political expression of progressive forces in Brazilian civil society. Even though with less fervour than in previous campaigns they have been engaged in the re-election campaign of Lula and/or PT candidates at other levels. Hence the thinking is that an end of the PT Cycle does not mean the end of the importance of the PT as an institutional political agent. It means, rather, its decline as a model for conducting social conflicts and that it will emphasize institutional action, entering into 'traditional politics' and respect for the 'rules of the game'.

Pablo Stefanoni and Hervé Do Alto

3
The emergence of
indigenous nationalism in Bolivia

Over the past few years Bolivia has been transforming itself into an extraordinary laboratory of collective action, social contestation and the building-up of political alternatives 'from below'. This experience has injected a non-negligible dose of sociological realism into all the theories about the articulation between the political and the social (including the ever-present problem of power) which are now discovering an empirical field for confirmation or refutation.

The basic thesis of this chapter is that in Bolivia a new popular-based indigenous nationalism has developed, which involves recognizing the breaks and continuities of the present process of change being experienced by this Andean Amazonian country. This led to the resounding electoral victory of the Movimiento al Socialismo–Instrumento Politico por la Soberanía de los Pueblos (MAS: Movement Towards Socialism as a Political Instrument for the Sovereignty of Peoples) on 18 December 2005 and the accession of the coca peasant farmer Evo Morales Ayma to the presidency.

What does this turning to the left in Bolivian politics after two decades of neoliberal hegemony consist of? What is the political, ideological and organizational nature of the 'political instrument' of the unions who are now in government? What are the possibilities and limitations of a successful post-neoliberal and democratizing project?

These are some of the questions that we shall try to answer, at least provisionally, in the following contribution, based on the 2005–006 period.[1]

Popular self-representation

The electoral victory of 18 December 2005 brought to power a new, nationalist left, which considered itself as the 'political instrument' of the peasant unions, the indigenous organizations and the popular urban bodies which, since 2000, have been the protagonists of a renewed cycle of contesting collective action capable of reflecting an ensemble of the main anti-neoliberal ideas. These ideas are based on recovering national sovereignty over natural resources and the 're-foundation' of the country by a sovereign constituent national assembly. At the same time they challenge the ethnically discriminatory character of the Bolivian State, established in 1825, which excluded 90 per cent of the population, identified as 'original peoples': Aymaras, Quechuas, Guaranis, etcetera. An innovatory form of relationships between the social and the political, based on self-representation and the projection of plebeian society in political and State terms, thus emerged through the powerful territorial union structures which have also been functioning as micro-governments in the agrarian communities and the poor quarters of the cities.

In a recent article, the sociologist and current vice-president, Álvaro García Linera, identified three stages in this process of accumulation of political power, which was only partly hindered by successive divisions within the popular movement, usually linked to struggles for the leadership: a first round of resistance in a local context (1987–95); a second round of expansion and search for alliances (1995–2001); then a round of consolidation and the offensive to take power (2001–06).[2]

In this process of expansion from the countryside to the town the coca peasant farmers (*cocaleros*) played a key role. They were able to turn their defence of coca cultivation, threatened by US programmes trying to eradicate it, into a national grievance against 'imperial interference' and for the defence of original cultures.

At the same time, a counterdiscourse developed, which challenged one of the hard-core issues in neoliberal policies that had been applied in Bolivia since 1985: the 'handing over' of natural resources – mainly hydrocarbons – to transnational capital.

This is a new nationalism whose protagonists are no longer the urban-educated middle classes who promoted *mestizaje* (mixed race) as a Bolivian ideal, as was done in the revolutionary nationalism of the

1950s, but the peasant and indigenous masses who were advancing a new idea of 'Bolivianness' that was anti-colonial, multi-cultural and inclusive. This is not, however, to deny that this 'plebeian nationalism' took over much of the old Bolivian nationalism, including the dichotomy between the people and the oligarchy, anti-imperialism, and the great importance given to the nationalization of natural resources as an engine for national development and the promotion of effective citizenship. Hence the 'recovery' of gas and oil has marked national policy since 2003: first, as the demand to the government of Carlos Mesa,[3] and then, as he refused to promulgate the law approved by Congress in May 2005,[4] the street fighting which, together with the resignation of Mesa, opened up the political-electoral transition that prepared the way for the victory of Morales.

A government of the social movements?

The comfortable victory of Evo Morales's MAS party – with almost 54 per cent of the votes – constituted one more step in this process of the popular accumulation of political power, while it was a real 'intellectual and moral' defeat for the neoliberal elites who had been governing the country since 1985. The ritual for the accession of Morales to the presidency was full of symbols signifying that the first indigenous president represented the turning of a page in Bolivian history. One of the events was a ceremony in the pre-Colombian temple of Tiwanaku, where Morales was proclaimed 'president of the indigenous peoples of the continent'.

At the same time the political and State experience of this 'movement of movements', with its corporate base, created new intellectual challenges concerning its democratizing possibilities and its ability to embark on processes of social empowerment or the construction of power 'from below'.

Can one talk of a government of social movements, in light of the first steps it has taken? We think that the answer is partly positive and partly negative. The current fragmentation of the social movements – and the lack of a party or any other form that institutionalizes the 'political instrument' – has enabled an extremely centralized model of decision making to emerge around the personality of Evo Morales. He operates through consultations between the government and the leaders of the social and union organizations who often reproduce, on a small scale, both clientelism and favouritism, which are far removed from the idealized image promoted by some theoreticians who have put the social movements on the good side of an uncrossable frontier that separates politics (impure) from the social (pure).

When there is such a corporative fragmentation of the political and social actors, it is up to the president to represent universality, as he is seen as the only person capable of developing the necessary overall vision for any innovatory political project. And, in this process, the leadership of Morales is contributing to the consolidation of the people as a political and social subject (beyond the multiplicity defended by the theoreticians of the multitude) in a permanent negotiation with the social movements. The form of leadership of Evo Morales reflects much of the charismatic leader (already many are talking about 'evismo') and it is not yet clear how to guarantee the public debate and social participation in a process of democratization from below which, according to the government, is being seen and promoted as a 'democratic and cultural revolution'.

Nevertheless, compared with classic populism where the relationship between the leader and the masses is direct (or, at least presented as such), the leadership of Morales is mediated by many corporative organizations and social movements to which he is accountable, in a Bolivian version of the 'command and obey mandate' of the Mexican Zapatistas. At important junctures, Evo Morales returns to the grassroots to renew the relationships that define his leadership. Morales thus has a high degree of authority, without however having a blank cheque permitting him to free himself from the union movements at the origin of the 'political instrument'. That is clear from each MAS congress, during which the Bolivian president carefully notes the proposals from the grassroots.

Andean capitalism or national capitalism?

There is the same tension – between the old and the new – in the socio-economic field: Vice-President García Linera's proposal for an 'Andean-Amazonian capitalism' has some innovatory features, together with more familiar ones.[5] His main thesis is that the erosion of the indigenous communal economies and the collapse (material and symbolic) of the old Bolivian working class have undermined the credibility of a socialist or post-capitalist project. So long as communal or 'scientific' socialism, or the articulation between the two, promoted by Marxist indigenism theorized by García himself, does not have subjects that are sufficiently powerful to advance them, 'Bolivia will remain capitalist for the next fifty to a hundred years'. However, this position does envisage a reduction in the old State capitalism. It is no longer a question, in a modernization process, of the modern economy absorbing the traditional one, but quite the contrary: it must be recognized that the pre-modern economy will remain valid and be supported by the State with the aim of creating the linkages with, but not subordinating it to, the modern pole of the dual economy that characterizes Bolivia.

Here a number of questions arise. What is the future, according to this proposal, for the old national capitalism, which has been tried with varying success by many nationalist-populist governments from the 1940s to the 1960s? Is this type of non-homogeneous developmentalism possible? Is capitalist expansion compatible with reinforcing the communities or does its very essence entail the dissolution of community ties? Can dependent capitalism be compatible with an emancipatory project?

The nationalization – with military occupation – decreed by the Bolivian government on 1 May 2006 was the first step in dismantling the neoliberal edifice that had been consolidated during the 1990s. The next steps will show whether there is a new postliberal economic dynamic which has taken over the old State capitalism (Keynesian), or whether it is just a new version of national capitalism, intended as a first step towards a greater socialization of the economy. Or, in other words, the old recipe of the revolution by stages, in an Andean-Amazonian wrapping, but with the same difficulty as in the past: the socialist stage never arrived.

Notes

1   Part of this analysis was developed in Pablo Stefanoni and Hervé Do Alto, *Evo Morales, de la coca al Palacio: Una oportunidad para la izquierda indígena*, La Paz, editorial Malatesta, 2006.

2   Álvaro García Linera, 'El evismo', *Soberania,* no. 2, La Paz, April 2006. [See also, by the same author, 'State crisis and popular power', *New Left Review,* London, January/February 2006 – *trans.*]

3   Carlos Mesa replaced Gonzalo Sánchez de Lozada when the latter fell from power in October 2003, during the so-called 'gas war'. Mesa tried to strike a fatal balance between the mobilized social sectors and the oil companies which, after a new wave of social conflicts, ended with his premature retirement from the presidency and opened up a transition period that concluded with the elections of 18 December 2005.

4   This law established a new system of hydrocarbon exploitation. The State took over the ownership of gas and oil 'at the head of the well' and imposed a combination of royalties and taxes of 50 per cent on production for the benefit of the Bolivian State. This law was the basis for the nationalization decree by Evo Morales on 1 May 2006.

5   'Le capitalisme andin-amazonien', *Le Monde Diplomatique* (Cône Sud edition), no. 79, Buenos Aires, January 2006.

Héctor Lucena

4
Venezuela: The workers' movement and the Bolivarian revolution

This chapter concentrates on the types of relationship between the workers' movement and the Bolivarian revolution. The heterogeneous nature of the workers' movement is a major factor to be taken into consideration. Not only are there strong ideological differences, but cleavages arise from the great variety of productive activities, which include businesses using state-of-the-art technology and finance, as well as a host of subsistence activities and others that create very little wealth. Also to be borne in mind is the fact that the relationships between the workers' movement and the State, in this case the Bolivarian revolution, are not the only conditioning factor: relationships with the employers as a body and as individual employers also play a role that is central to the movement's existence.

This chapter will analyse the ups and downs of the relationships between the workers' movement and the Bolivarian revolution: the advances allowed by the government, but also the reversals, and the reactions of the movement. It could be described as a zigzag approach: governmental projects put forward and then blocked; proposals presented by the movement which received no governmental response. At the same time I shall examine the genuine progress that has been achieved outside and independently of governmental action.

I am aware that the brevity of this chapter makes it difficult to meet all the analytical requirements of such a task, particularly in the case of a country like Venezuela which is at present experiencing a heady ferment. Further analyses will have to await another discussion.

Basic changes in the relationships within the workers' movement

The trade-union situation before Hugo Chávez came to power was virtually stagnant. Since Black Friday in 1983, wages had been declining, the percentage of the unemployed ran into double figures and the informal economy grew apace. Trade unionism had maintained its conquests in only a very few sectors. Hence, when Chávez, the presidential candidate in 1998, announced that he was going to confront the trade unionism organized in the Confederación de Trabajadores de Venezuela (CTV), he met with wide support, including from the employers. The latter saw the possibility of weakening the trade-union movement (even if the CTV had lost much of its capacity to mobilize its members because of its bureaucracy). Then Chávez came to power and implemented measures that weakened the CTV trade-union movement. These measures included the suspension of State economic support, elimination of union leaders from their responsibilities in public enterprises, suspension of trade- union directives throughout the unions' structures, calling for and implementing a union referendum, and the submission of union elections to the National Electoral Council.

Although successive elections enabled Chávez to reinforce his power over a relatively short period of time, the trade-union referendum and elections turned out to be blunders. Thus encouraged, the CTV, together with business leaders and opposition parties, organized a series of mobilizations that were highly successful compared with those of recent decades,

However the CTV is not the only expression of the workers' movement. There are other, alternative trade-union organizations: some not confederated but others that, in spite of belonging to the CTV, openly took their distance from their leaders. And, as the unnatural relationships between the CTV and the employers became more evident, in 2003 there emerged a new trade union (the Union Nacional de los Trabajadores – UNT), whose aim was to be the direct interlocutor of trade unionists with the government.

Up until that point governmental action, rather than supporting the workers' movement, was to create an appropriate climate to bring about certain changes in the trade-union movement. The shocks administered to the CTV bureaucracy enabled left-wing unionists who had formerly been repressed to win a greater margin of manoeuvre.

They also led certain leaders who had previously been active in the social democratic and Christian socialist parties to opt for the UNT, thus reducing the membership of the traditional trade-union organization. This phase has seen the strengthening of the workers' movement, which has rediscovered its mobilization capacity. And the conflictual relationship between the government and the employers, before and after the *coup d'état* of 2002, has enabled the workers' movement to develop without fearing an alliance between the owners and the public authorities to repress their activities, as often happened in the past. If such progress seems modest enough, it is very important for the workers' movement, whose structures are obliged to adopt democratic processes. This has greatly helped to improve its present capacity to mobilize people.

The governmental measures taken in the political and economic fields have been supported by the workers' movement. However, a closer look reveals that the centralizing and presidential style of government has had the result that the workers' movement, as organized in the UNT, has been largely supporting actions after the event. Decisions on wage policy, the formulation of laws and management of the main public enterprises, receive UNT support although they reflect decisions taken elsewhere. The workers' movement can generate enthusiasm and get people on to the streets, but it must have its own agenda and actively participate in formulating policies.

Risks and new problems

The trade-union movement in Venezuela is now developing in a very particular, if not contradictory situation, as the structures of production have considerably diminished in recent years. This revival of the trade-union movement during a period of entrepreneurial restructuring, which tends to make union organization more difficult, is no mean undertaking. In these revolutionary Chávez years, Venezuela is more dependent on oil for revenue than formerly, as there is a continual process of deindustrialization. Also, the jobs created by public financial incentives are in small businesses, micro-enterprises and cooperatives, often replacing jobs that have been unionized and made subject to collective bargaining. All this can only render the future of worker organizations more difficult.

In the small businesses the situation is in fact very delicate. Most trade unionism in Venezuela has in the past been based on individual factories or plants. But certain material conditions are necessary to guarantee the survival of trade-union organization. On the other hand, it is the micro-enterprises and cooperatives that are being politically and financially incentivized and given priority, through public tenders and contracts. So now many private and public businesses are converting themselves in order to fit into this framework, frequently contravening labour laws as they disguise themselves as cooperatives when in fact they are businesses. Moreover, in order to obtain public subsidies they often have recourse to corruption. These are some of the challenges facing the workers' movement.

Flexibility and public enterprises

The changes that have been put in place by the Bolivarian revolution are mainly due to public initiative. It should be remembered that the Venezuelan State is very bureaucratic. It is an oil state that enjoys exceptional revenues, which helps it to amass a colossal fortune. Thus it can count on public funds to achieve its projects, however diversified they may be. So it is with the creation of jobs: it is no accident that most of the jobs that have been created are in the public sector. Since Chávez came to power, no fewer than 1.6 million workers have been found jobs. However in most of the public enterprises the measures taken in the field of labour relations have not produced the desired effects. It is true that certain neoliberal measures, particularly as regards privatization, have been checked, the privatizing of enterprises has become rarer, while the flexibility of work is limited. But as far as flexibility is concerned, there are two important exceptions, which constitute a serious pitfall for the workers' movement. As has already been mentioned, in the drive to promote cooperatives pseudo-cooperatives have become dominant, while the anti-flexibility measures do not apply to employment in the public sector, which is where a large majority of the formal workers are to be found.

Demands, the work space and the living space

The workers' movement has broadened the scope of its demands, which has in turn helped it to strengthen its activities. Traditionally its claims were confined to the workplace, where trade unionists drew up their platforms for action and fought to implement them. But the space in which they lived, in their communities, in their neighbourhoods, was ignored. Now, with the increasing deterioration of infrastructure, declining services, lack of security and the degradation of living standards, a whole range of proposals for organizing communal social activities has developed.

Formerly, unionized workers did not participate in the informal economy, which involves the majority of the population whose working conditions are undefined, volatile and unstable. Their living space thus remains central to their concerns, indeed it often coincides with their working space, through the economic activities generated by the neighbourhood and the community in general. An important task for the various sectors of the workers' movement is to bring together those who work in the modern sector with those who work in the informal economy, who are more difficult to organize through the nature of their productive activities.

Manolo García

5

Reinvigorated indigenous and popular movements tackle Guatemala's huge inequalities

In Guatemala, the great inequalities in access to the means of production and the unfair distribution of income keep about 57 per cent of the population in poverty and 28 per cent of them in extreme poverty. At the present time it seems very likely that these social indices will worsen, above all for the indigenous rural population in the western highlands.

The coffee crisis caused the loss of 80,000 jobs in the agricultural sector, while there has been a reduction in the human development indices in the western highlands where most of the poor rural indigenous population live. To these must be added the destruction caused by the tropical storm Stan which, in the south-west of the country, destroyed much of the production capacity of the rural economy and created lasting damage to investment projects.

There will also be negative consequences for the economy when the free trade treaty with the United States comes into force in 2006 According to a study by the Inter-American Development Bank (IBD), this will affect 53 per cent of rural households through the introduction of subsidized agricultural products from the United States. With this agreement, some 600,000 rural households which up until now had been more or less self-sufficient, thanks to their subsistence crops, will need some form of assistance to cope with the new situation. The agreement will above all introduce some 996 North American agricultural products into the Guatemalan market, all exempt from customs duty: 427 will have direct access to the market, 104 in five years' time, 143 in 10 years' time, 180 when the treaty comes into force, and the rest within 20 years' time.

Two other measures are also having a negative effect on the popular economy, mainly in the rural west of the country. These are the steps taken by the United States to limit the number of migrants: an unprecedented criminalization of people without documents and a proposal to tax the sending of money back from the US to the migrant's country of origin. This remission of earnings is estimated to amount to no less than US\$3.4 billion for 2006 and it cushions tens of thousands of families from falling into absolute poverty and destitution. This sum is considerably greater than the income earned from any export products and has been an important stimulus in transforming local economies by facilitating survival as well as small-scale social investment (education), trade (including the purchase of vehicles and means of communication) and infrastructure (housing).

Another factor that weakens the Guatemalan economy is the rise in oil prices, which has caused a spectacular increase in the price of fuel products and thus of transport, electric energy, propane gas, and also the housewife's shopping basket. Nor is the Guatamalan economy ready to make good the deficit in employment. On the contrary, hardly 20 per cent of the 125,000 young people who annually come on to the labour market find jobs that are more or less stable. And this climate of economic uncertainty, which encourages many young people to take to *pandillas* (gangs of delinquents) and criminality will not be remedied by the limited social expenditure, a few initiatives taken by the State, civil organizations and the private sector (but poorly coordinated between them), or a limited offer of education, which will partially benefit only certain sectors of society – and not the poor.

In a situation that continues to deteriorate, it is likely that the middle and lower middle classes, composed of waged workers, self-employed workers and employees who live in urban areas that are increasingly threatened by the criminality and extortion practices of the *pandillas,* will increasingly turn, through their survival instinct, to extremely harsh and conservative ideologies and will in particular support the restriction, if not the elimination, of civil liberties. In addition, because they are unable to participate in the globalization dynamic, the more volatile local firms are becoming involved in the criminal economy, particularly serving to screen money-laundering operations. This illustrates the social decomposition of the society, which affects all classes of the population.

The building of a social movement that is plural, indigenous and popular

After the reversals provoked by the repression of the war years, the globalization process and the various regional mega-projects seem to have had just one positive consequence. They have encouraged the emergence of new alliances between the popular movements, which have led to many mobilizations, motivated mainly by participants' fear at seeing what meagre natural resources still exist disappear or pass into the hands of others. This phase in which the peasant and popular movements have come together at the national level, but also at a Central American level, is a symbol of hope. For it could eventually create a veritable dynamic of common mobilizations in the country against the transnationalization process induced by the Plan Puebla Panamá, the mega-projects and the free trade treaty with the United States.

The communities and the poor sectors who are being made precarious by these processes, for the most part the indigenous and rural people, and women, see their lives and future possibilities threatened still more than in the past. The uncertainty and covert repression that have dominated the country since the onset of the armed conflict at the end of the 1970s still continue. The dilemma that the population has faced over the past 500 years – should they submit or oppose the dominating powers? – poses itself once again. Thus there has been renewed interest in popular education, organization, coordination of starting-up programmes and projects, reinforcement of the local authorities and participation in public decision making, both in government and at the community, municipal, departmental and national levels. The question of autonomy *vis-à-vis* the government and the true strength of community decisions, for example in choosing the local authorities, are currently the causes of this new social tension. And it has been the young women and the indigenous representatives who, because of the quality of their leaders at the local level, have played an important role in this process.

Before the Spaniards invaded the country, the Maya calendars had foretold a dark age, but also a renaissance, with the reconstruction of a new era of peace and progress. Inspired by these prophecies and their own survival instincts, the leaders of many communities and social organizations now hope that the future will bring hope and a new breath of life, confronted as they are by the destructive effects of neoliberal globalization, which are weighing heavily on them: increased poverty, insecurity and violence, rising oil prices, US military interventions in the Muslim world, climate catastrophes and so on. Some of the Maya leaders nourish the belief that this historical period that has proved so ruinous for their people will end in the coming years.

The organizational process started by developing a coordination of municipalities, including both communities and social and religious organizations, both of whom are trying to reinforce community organization. They are also trying to work on the more important coordinations at the departmental and regional levels. The municipal, indigenous and ecclesiastical authorities have begun to realize the need to support these local forces, even to participate in their activities. There is no doubt that they will have a significant influence on the development of new programmes and projects, as well as the reinforcement of local economies and the coming elections.

Recently the rural communities and local associations have been coming closer to the most influential popular, social and political organizations at the national level. The latter have realized the importance of community action, of integrating it at all levels and of the need to link up the mobilizations, even if there is still a minority elite which, in the social NGOs as in the indigenous movement, continues to take over and monopolize contacts, participation and national and international information.

Thus the repression that these organizations suffer, particularly from the government, can act as a brake on the gradual process of creating a social counter-power. Lately, the national authorities severely repressed the communities and peasants of Sololá who stopped an engine destined for a mining enterprise in the western part of the country. The government has also removed the communities and peasant organizations who were occupying agricultural lands that were not being exploited by their 'legal' owners.

Within the indigenous movement, the creation of the Maquib Kiej organization aims at restoring the unity of the movement, after the many disagreements and tactical errors that caused the disintegration of the Copmagnua. This deprived the indigenous peoples of an important means for making claims and pressing for the application of the peace agreement of 1996 which has now been practically forgotten.

The constitution of the peasant movement, indigenous and popular, whose image is strong and unified, is also significant for several reasons. It is the result of the disappointed hopes of trade-union circles, the sellers at the Terminal market, organizations of elderly people, representatives of community radios, teacher and peasant leaders, who confront a government that is incapable of giving satisfactory answers to their demands.

At the outset this movement announced a timetable of actions in the framework of what it called the 'national and popular Maya uprising'. But these mobilizations were suspended because of the opening of the 'national dialogue'. It is likely, however, that if this dialogue with the government fails, the actions that have been planned will gradually be taken up again, threatening to take the form of an uprising on a national scale. For the moment, however, there does not seem enough unity and mobilization to carry out such a movement on a South American scale.

Confronted by this growth in popular struggles, the Guatemalan government has reacted by timidly opening spaces for dialogue. But it is more than probable that this will not lead anywhere or, worse, that it will end up, as in the past, by co-opting the social, indigenous and peasant leaders and even the former guerrilla fighters, who will justify their new positions by zealously defending governmental policies.[1]

In Guatemala today, what is evident is that the relationships of subordination that prevailed between the organizations and networks of the social movements on the one hand, and the political organizations, on the other, is gradually disappearing, giving way to a social movement that is more autonomous, even though there continue to be groups and elites that try to centralize and dominate it. This kind of leader makes organic convergences difficult within a sector that includes an increasingly large number of people, associations and professional and intellectual organizations involved in the social struggle in many ways. True, they are often still dispersive, but they constitute the ferment of an important social force for the future.

Note

1   Thus there is a coordination of official services occupied by indigenous 'representatives'. And, within the present neoliberal government of the conservative president Oscar Berger, is the former indigenous mayor of Quetzaltenango,

the second largest town of the country, Rigoberto Quemé, who, at the primary elections of the Great National Alliance (GANA, the coalition that brought Berger to power in 2003), put forward his candidature for the presidential elections of 2007. This indigenous leader has, however, denounced the attempts of business circles to instrumentalize his participation.

Maristella Svampa

6
Argentina: The Kirchner method and Peronism's force of inertia

Argentina is at present going through a period full of paradoxes. On the one hand there is a lot of mobilization through a combination of non-institutional collective actions, the tendency to take to non-conventional direct action, and the development of participatory structures involving peoples' assemblies. These three types of action have given rise to a host of organizations, ranging from the movement of the unemployed (the *piqueteros*), now much vilified, factories that have been taken over and trade unions undertaking new forms of action, to the multisectoral assemblies in defence of housing, peasant and indigenous organizations; and collective actions protesting against insecurity. On the other hand, there is the political institutional scene, with the hegemony of the governing Peronist party, as illustrated by the concentration of power in the hands of the president, Nestor Kirchner, who was elected in 2003. This has resulted in fragilizing certain political parties and causing the decline of others, as well as the government co-opting many unemployed workers' organizations and human rights associations.

This paradoxical situation, which can be seen in the existence of both confrontation and cooperation between the social actors and the government, is taking place at a time of economic recovery and fiscal surplus which have reduced unemployment (now standing at 11.4 per cent), but also led to a widening gap between social classes. Whereas ten years ago the richest 10 per cent earned 20 times more than the poorest 10 per cent, currently the ratio is over 27:1. It is, however, clear that the present government has favoured the emergence of an antiliberal Latin American space, in which governments and social actors converge. Nevertheless, while the political scene has greatly changed these last few years, as can be seen from all the critical political debates, the neoliberal model – and the political regime that helped to install it – is robustly healthy.

First of all, one of the most striking recent developments is undeniably the institutionalization of the different social organizations and the incorporation into the government of many *piquetero* leaders belonging to the national populist tradition and associated with Peronism. The counter-effect of this is the disciplining and demonizing of the organizations of the unemployed that are against the government. In fact, in spite of the government's declaration that it 'will not repress', there has been a policy to stigmatize mobilizing organizations and to 'bring them to justice'.

This campaign, which was carried out from 2003 to 2005 with the support of the most important communications media and the most influential traditional sectors of society, resulted in the anti-*piquetero* consensus that prevails in Argentina today. The results are evident: during 2006 there was a sharp decline in actions by the *piqueteros*, especially in Buenos Aires. Similarly the stigmatization process intensified the fragmentation of the militants.

Nevertheless the struggles of the *piqueteros* have continued and even extended into the oil enclaves controlled by the transnationals. The two regions considered to be the centres of the *piquetero* movement, Neuquén and northern Salta, have recently been joined by the province of Santa Cruz in southern Patagonia, where President Kirchner was governor for many years. There the conflicts with the workers and the unemployed intensified between 2004 and early 2006, leading to the imprisonment of *piqueteros* and union delegates, while the region was militarized through the deployment of troops, the national gendarmerie, provincial police and special intervention groups. In the end, after denunciations of human rights violations, the conflict in Santa Cruz was pacified by the oil workers' claims being satisfied and social assistance funds being distributed to the unemployed. Kirchner also replaced the governor of the province.

Second, trade union conflict has significantly increased. As could be expected, the consolidation of Kirchner's leadership helped to realign Peronist unionism, which had been dominated by the Confederación General del Trabajo (CGT). It should be recalled that, in the 1990s, this confederation endorsed the neoliberal reforms. Kirchner's policies also had a serious effect on the political orientation of the Central de Trabajadores Argentinos (CTA), created in 1994 and known for its critical and anti-neoliberal views. In fact, with the reactivation of the national populist tradition, the CTA is passing through a period of considerable ambiguity because of internal divisions, particularly as certain of its leaders support official policies.

In 2005, however, there were three times as many worker conflicts as in 2004: 819 union conflicts compared with 249. Although most of these demanded wage increases, a good number denounced precariousness and are trying to reduce the disparities in wages between workers in the same sector – disparities that were promoted by subcontracting and the wage flexibility policy imposed in the 1990s. Nor should it be forgotten that, according to official statistics, the informal sector has considerably increased over the last few years, now affecting 44.3 per cent of the active population, while wages have diminished by 30 per cent compared with 2001.

The most striking union conflicts have been organized by internal coordinating bodies and sometimes without the authorization of the recognized unions (including the CTA itself). They have included actions by workers in the telephone sector (call centres depending on Telefónica Argentina), in transport (the metro) and in public health (hospitals). All this led to the creation of a new union coordinating body, the Movimiento Intersindical Clasista, which brings together the grassroots left that openly claims its affinity with the organizations of the independent *piqueteros*.

Third, there is an important movement of workers who are managing factories and who continue to struggle, using judicial and legislative means, to obtain an expropriation law and recognition as cooperatives. There are now some 170 factories that have been taken over, involving about 12,000 workers. Unlike the *piquetero* experience, the expropriation of factories met with considerable sympathy and social support, which was essential for its expansion and consolidation. Apart from a few cases, such as the ceramics firm Zanón-Fasinpat[1] in Patagonia and the very central Hotel Bauen in Buenos Aires, the expropriation of factories has been opposed only feebly by the State, although its reactions have not always been the same. In fact the State encouraged and supported the process, first by establishing the National Institute for

Associations and the Social Economy and then by facilitating the establishment of cooperatives, definitive expropriation and temporary cession (two years) in favour of the workers. The occupied factories are indeed openly becoming institutionalized in spite of major obstacles caused by lack of support for the marketing of their products and the organizational fragmentation of the sector. Of the four streams that form the movement, two have close ties with the government, their leaders having declared themselves *oficialistas*.

Of quite a different order is the increase in insecurity which is to be seen in different forms and at various levels because of an evident lack of State control and regulation, resulting in lack of protection for citizens. An accident that moved the whole country was the death of 194 young people through a fire in the Cromagnon disco in Buenos Aires. Although the place had a capacity for only 1,200 people, when the accident occurred, in December 2004, more than 4,000 people were present. It was soon discovered that none of the safety regulations of the building had been respected, and the 'Cromagnon massacre' came to be seen as a tragic example of an excluding socio-economic model, showing up the negligence of the authorities responsible for the safety of young people. Shortly afterwards the families and survivors of the tragedy organized themselves to insist that justice be done and that those directly or indirectly responsible be brought to trial. The pressure of the families of the victims, as well as the investigations carried out, highlighted the responsibility of Aníbal Ibarra, mayor of the capital, who were removed from office in March 2006 for 'poor execution of his duties'.

Another important development in Argentina has been the emergence of environmental demands. As in other Latin American countries, these mobilizations have centred on defence of habitats, and protection of biodiversity and natural nonrenewable resources, in light of the depredations of the transnationals. Many actions in various regions of the country have called into question the development of toxic mining using open-face explosions and treatment with cyanide. As with the politicization that started in 2002 and also in the 1990s when there were community uprisings because of the crisis and the dismantling of the regional economies, these environmental actions have become multisectoral and take the form of assembly participation (assemblies of the self-invited).

The environmental conflict that has had the greatest national and international impact is the protest of the people of Gualeguaychú, in the

Entre Ríos province, against the installation of paper industries that had been authorized by the Uruguayan government. The local people on the Argentinian side of the river came together in assembly and began their demands by denouncing the danger of pollution, which would be the product of the 'accumulation effect' of the installation of two large paper factories on the Uruguayan side of the river. Having received no response from the authorities, they took to direct action, organizing huge processions across the frontiers in 2005 and 2006. The demand of the local people (called *neopiqueteros* by some of the press because of the way they used marches and picketing) was supported by the national government. Its probable aim was to make capital out of a large social mobilization that seemed to involve no internal political costs. Nevertheless, the conflict became very complex and uncertain of outcome. Then there was a confrontation between local and global actors which ended with Argentina and Uruguay forced into political and diplomatic negotiations. Thus the conflict tended to be couched in nationalist terms, which created increasing tensions between the two governments.

During 2006 the controversy led to two legal proceedings. One, presented by Argentina to the International Court of Justice at The Hague on the question of environmental pollution, was decided in favour of Uruguay. The other was the case opened at the Arbitration Tribunal of MERCOSUR (Mercado Común del Sur), in which Uruguay denounced 'the lack of appropriate measures by the Argentinian State' concerning the marches at the frontier and demanded economic compensation. Surprisingly, in this second trial the Argentinian government took on the defence of the 'assembly members' of Gualeguachú, insisting that 'freedom of circulation' came after 'freedom of expression' – an argument contrasting with the government's position on the road and street barricades that were organized by other associations, especially the unemployed, which resulted in protest 'criminalization' trials. Thus, from 1997 to date, there have been some 4,000 trials, many of them of people having participated in road blockages. Under Kirchner's government there has even been an increase in the trials resulting from social conflict, which landed various demonstrators and activists in prison.

These struggles and trials are taking place against a Latin American background in which neoliberalism is being challenged and continental alliances are being tried out. The Argentinian government has known how to exploit this new Latin American conjuncture. The continental political scene was reinforced by the latest summit of MERCOSUR, which took place in Cordoba (Argentina) in July 2006, and saw the entry of Venezuela into the organization. This divided the militant camp: there were numerous tensions and much ambivalence among the social movements that oppose Kirchner, but great enthusiasm among the *oficialistas*. In this context, the question of the political stance of the Kirchner government has become a key issue, given that almost all the social organizations and movements expect that future challenges will take place in this new space, especially if MERCOSUR adopts a more political-economic line.

A number of self-organization forms of social life – including *piquetero* organizations and the classic human rights groups – have become integrated into the government sphere. Nevertheless, time will be needed to evaluate the extent to which the institutionalization option leads to greater citizen participation. For the time being, progress has so far been made in 'memory politics', that is, condemnation of the violations of human rights during the last military dictatorship. But, as a consequence, the organizations not only renounce their autonomy and promote political demobilization. They also tend to develop ties of subordination and political dependency on the leader (Kirchner) – which is indeed in the Peronist tradition.

However, we should not forget that in spite of the array of *oficialista* organizations, there is a solid collection of anti-capitalist social organizations that are critical of the present government and they are well organized in national and global networks. Also the capacity of the party currently in power to co-opt can be weakened by the continuing emergence of new demands, which invariably take the form of direct action and assembly organization as a form of expression that overflows the fragile institutional channels.

Finally, ambiguities, tensions and double-speak are common in both discourse and practice, with a horizon that is open to new dynamics and challenges that will be much influenced by the new forms of social mobilization, as against the hegemony of Peronism.

Note

1   *Fasinpat* is an acronym for *fábrica sin patron* (ownerless factory).

Guillermo Almeyra

7
Mexico is becoming Latinamericanized

For many years Mexico was the exception in Latin America. Not only has it not experienced military dictatorship since the victory of the Mexican Revolution at the beginning of the twentieth century, it also had a State party system which, since the 1930s, received a virtual consensus from the population until the 1980s. The PRI (Partido Revolucionario Institucional) included capitalist sectors on the right but also workers and peasants on the social left, extending to revolutionary socialist nationalists. Because of Mexico's relative social tranquillity it served as a buffer that protected the southern frontier of the United States.

As from the 1980s the globalization pursued by international finance capital destroyed the foundations of this anomalous political situation and transformed the country and its institutions. The great State enterprises – except for oil and the Electricity Federal Commission – were privatized and most of them passed into the hands of the transnationals. So did the banks. The government was changed into a team of entrepreneurs or their representatives (currently led by Vicente Fox, former president of Coca-Cola, Mexico) who gave priority to repaying the debt and financial services. The internal market and development were thrust aside and the country became almost totally dependent on food imports, as well as industrial goods and technology from the United States, while it exported oil and labour to its northern neighbour.

The rural sector, which has been half destroyed, now represents 15 per cent of the population and is the most affected by emigration and the prices of US food commodities (which are highly subsidized). It also suffers from the deterioration of its natural resources and increasing shortages of water. Small and medium businesses have been displaced by branches of the transnationals so that when someone says 'Mexico exports...' they mean that Nissan, Volkswagen, Ford and other such industries are exporting.

The inevitable social protest took the form of an uprising in 1994, coinciding with the coming into force of the North American Free Trade Agreement (NAFTA) with the United States of America and Canada. The uprising was led by an indigenous movement in Chiapas and its Zapatista Army for National Liberation (EZLN). This movement still continues today, serving as an alternative power to the State through autonomous municipalities, organized in *caracoles* (snails) and run by renewable *juntas de buen gobierno* (commissions for good government), which are elected in participatory assemblies. However this protest did not remain isolated and confined to Chiapas: it stimulated the extension of other forms of autonomy in other indigenous communities that were not run by the EZLN, a massive peasant mobilization, and serious worker and popular conflicts (which, in Atenco, prevented the construction of a new airport for the city of Mexico and led to a huge struggle that was ferociously repressed in May 2006).

The massive emigration of more than a million workers a year is also a sign of this social protest, although a passive one. In fact, there are no great social movements (the EZLN is in a minority position even in Chiapas and is not strongly supported in the rest of the country) except that expressed through emigration. The trade-union leadership was used to giving way to the government, although the breaking up of relations between the two indicates the strength of the pressure from below.

This increasingly large pressure from the grassroots expressed itself in 2006 through the huge mobilization of people supporting the candidature of Andrés Manuel López Obrador (AMLO) to the presidency. Each time the movement gets bigger: in the last one, the largest in the country's history, one and a half million people participated. Defence of the legal victories of the Mexican Revolution, through legal and peaceful means, combines with direct action (such as the bloody encounters with the police and the prolonged occupation of the city of Oaxaca by 70,000 teachers on strike).

The presidential elections took place in this context. On the one hand there was the Partido de Acción Nacional (the old right-wing party: ultraclerical, entrepreneurial and pro-imperialist) and the PRI (which is divided and has lost much of its prestige), and on the other there is the Partido de la Revolución Democrática (PRD), most of whose leadership is corrupt and which on all the most important issues has voted with the right. However, among its capitalist policies it does include nationalist and distribution objectives. And it calls for popular mobilization when there is no alternative. It is opposed to the nationalization of the oil industry and electric energy, and talks of defending the development of the domestic market. Its candidate, AMLO, although he does not endanger the system, is a threat to the regime, to the concentration of wealth, and to racism. He is therefore denounced as 'dangerous' by the government and the right. And the latter, over the last two years, have been preparing fraudulent elections to avoid a victory by AMLO. The authorities first tried to imprison López Obrador to prevent his candidature. A gigantic social demonstration dissuaded them. The government and the right then used all the powers of the State and huge sums of money to manipulate public opinion, in collaboration with the large television and information corporations.

In a country whose culture is conservative, where bishops still play an important role and where those who do not vote or who vote for PAN or PRI amount to 60 per cent of the population, and in the absence of a large mobilization of people and a real, mass-based left-wing party, PAN was able to increase its share of the votes to 30 per cent, thanks to support from television and the State apparatus.

However, this was not enough to beat Andrés Manuel López Obrador, who won the elections, succeeding in doubling the usual vote of his party, particularly in the poor and most densely populated districts in the centre and south of the country. Then his opponents in power were forced to have recourse to the old, well-tried method of direct fraud by changing the results at the ballot boxes. As a result, a huge legal and peaceful protest against the fraudulent elections and the re-election of the PAN took place when the government, the establishment and all the right wing decided not to give way to pressure and to hang on to power at all costs.

Demonstrations of a million and a half or two million people are a risk but not a direct threat. There has not been a strike by workers against the fraud, nor have the streets been occupied by peasants who have been cheated. And, in any case, 35 or 40 per cent is still less than the 60 per cent that actively or passively support the regime which at the time of writing has not given way.

Nevertheless social pressures have divided the capitalist sector. This is not only because two partisan blocs are in confrontation (the pre-capitalist PRD and the nationalist part of the PRI against PAN and the right-wing, also in the PRI), but also because of the confrontation between small and medium industry in their chambers of commerce on one side, and the large exporting foreign corporations and the banks on the other. Furthermore the situation has created serious tensions within the armed forces between the nationalists and the military who defend, at all costs, their privileges and their alliance with drug dealers. Most important, all this has given an extraordinary political lesson to the population, who have become aware of the real role of the State institutions, the elections and 'justice'. As a result direct action is being prepared, legitimate but not legal, through self-organization and autonomy.

'The other campaign' organized during 2006 by the EZLN did not attract the support hoped for by its promoters because, as its name indicates, it was carried out on an anti-election and abstentionist platform. The Zapatista Sub-Commandante Marcos and his partisans, especially those from the student extreme left, wrongfooted the social movements, which supported *zapatismo* but would not take orders from it. They decided to vote for AMLO, together with the workers and the poor who were mobilizing on a massive scale to vote for the PRD candidate. Marcos carried out anarchistic and populistic agitation against 'the rich' and 'the corrupt' but his campaign in no way tackled the great national problems. Nor, in fact, did the PRD, which however saw the vote as a solution, while Marcos favoured abstention, thus benefiting the PAN.

'The other campaign' did not, however, speak of Cuba, Venezuela, MERCOSUR, the Middle East, imperialism and preventive war. Marcos even advised people 'not to look towards Bolivia' as he was afraid of the negative consequences for his own policies of the example of the Bolivian social movements which, without giving up their struggle and while remaining themselves, won the elections and imposed the holding of a constituent assembly to change the country. Thus 'the other campaign' had little influence with its call for abstention – indeed, there was less abstention than usual, given the importance and the polarization of the elections. Unfortunately, however, this separated his followers from the main body of the workers, which have been the first social movement at the national level, with a political line for more than seventy years. This provoked division and crisis in 'the other campaign' at the same time that, in Chiapas, the autonomous experiments and the commissions for good government were paralysed by having to comply with the decision for a 'red alert' by Marcos and the EZLN.

What can happen in the immediate future if the government imposes the PAN candidate, Felipe Calderón? The massive and determined protest movement does not have an organizational base. It is probable that the leadership of the PRD (which has more banks and money than ever before) will accept the governmental decision and lead the parliamentary and legal opposition, with support from a wing of the PRI. An illegitimate and illegal government will have to govern against the wishes of the poor, the oppressed and the workers, who will probably use their own organizations. There will be national strikes by workers and peasants, popular struggles and mobilization, above all if PAN makes labour regulations 'flexible' in favour of the 'free market' and privatizes the oil industry – as it probably will try to do, given its arrogance and racism. There is plenty of room for manoeuvre for the left, which can emerge from the crisis of 'the other campaign' and the redefinition of the groups supporting the PRD.

Part of the armed forces does not agree to participating in the dirty work that would be involved in a massive and bloody repression. The PAN must consider carefully before mobilizing the army on the orders of a right-wing government. The war in the Middle East, the possibility of an increase in the economic difficulties of the United States, the rejection of Mexican migrant workers, the example of MERCOSUR and Bolivia: all these developments should give pause for thought. In Argentina, Fernando de la Rúa obtained a genuine majority, unlike Calderón. And yet he was forced to flee by helicopter. In Bolivia, too, Gonzalo Sánchez had, in all legality, beaten Evo Morales (who had then received 20 per cent of the vote), but he is now in exile in the United States. Not even the assassination of demonstrators could keep him in power.

We return to what I said at the beginning: Mexico is becoming 'Latinamericanized' and elections are not definitive in an acute class struggle. Especially when they are fraudulent.

Raúl Zibechi

8
The social movement and
the left-wing government in Uruguay

In July 2002 the economic and financial crisis that shook Uruguay as a direct consequence of the collapse of its large Argentinian neighbour reached its apogee. The 'country risk' rose from 220 to 3,000 between the months of January and July. The public, having lost all confidence in the financial system, withdrew no less than 45 per cent of their bank savings, while the price of the dollar doubled in a few weeks. The year ended with a drop of 10 per cent in the GDP, which was barely half what it had been three years previously. The unemployment rate was close to the record of 20 per cent of the active population. Almost 40 per cent of Uruguayans found themselves below the poverty threshold.

However, in contrast with other countries of the continent, this violent economic and social crisis did not upset the political system. On the contrary, in Uruguay, the political left – the Frente Amplio (Broad Front), together with the trade-union association (PIT-CNT), the main organized social force – avoided an open confrontation with the government of Jorge Battle and, even at the worst moment of the crisis, ensured that the country remained governable. In fact, the explicit aim of the left was to transfer the crisis into the electoral arena in order to win the elections of October 2004. This explains why the social struggles of 2003 and 2004 were carefully channelled by the trade-union and party leaders, respecting a long Uruguayan tradition which throughout the twentieth century considered political stability as an end in itself.

Consultation with the population has been one way of channeling the protests. At the height of the economic and financial crisis, the social movement and the Frente Amplio worked hard to obtain the 600,000 signatures (20 per cent of the electoral roll) required to organize a referendum to prevent the State oil company (Ancap) from receiving private capital. This consultation, held in December 2003, ended with a first victory: 62 per cent of participants voted for annulment of the law approved by Battle's neoliberal government.

Flushed with this success, the social left organized another plebiscite a few months later. 2004 was electoral year and the plebiscite therefore took place at the same time as the campaign of the Frente Amplio, with the aim of opposing the privatization of water and insisting that it was an inalienable public good. Once again, the left was successful, with almost two-thirds of the votes against privatization. While in Argentina and Bolivia the question of privatization gave rise to mobilizations that destabilized the political system, in Uruguay the issue was played out on the political/electoral scene. The institutional framework was only ignored when marginalized sectors of the urban periphery of Montevideo sacked a dozen supermarkets. These actions, which were violently repressed by the police, were vigorously criticized across the political spectrum.

When the left-wing government presided over by Tabaré Vázquez came to power on 1 March 2005, the socio-political context for the social movements changed considerably. It was above all the trade unions who benefited from the new situation. Tripartite (State-employers-unions) negotiating mechanisms were established by the new government to give a legal framework for discussions on work relations and wages. In this favourable climate, trade-union membership rose considerably (by almost 70,000 new members, an increase of 60 per cent) and more than 300 unions were created. While the number of strikes greatly diminished, occupations of factories were more frequent and became the main means of confronting the intransigence of the employer organizations. The abrogation by the government of a decree that had allowed workers to be expelled if they were occupying their enterprise made such occupations a major means for unions to resolve conflicts.

In this new context, other movements took up various positions, which were often contradictory. The movement against the privatization of water was mobilized mainly to see that the results of the referendum were respected. But this mobilization soon seemed useless, given that the new authorities seemed disposed to respect the results, so that there was a decline in the activities of the National Commission for the Defence of Water and Life.

The human rights movement redoubled its activities when the government started excavating the remains of those who had disappeared during the military dictatorship and who had been buried in military barracks. The success of the authorities – for the first time some human remains were found – far from putting an end to the movement, caused it to press further in its demands for truth and justice. The social movement was also quick to react, vigorously denouncing the criminalization of the protest when, on the day of the Free Trade of the Americas Agreement (FTAA) Summit at Mar del Plata, numerous demonstrators were injured or arrested by the police in the centre of Montevideo.

Other sectors whose mobilization was worthy of note were the movements of the unemployed and the poor inhabitants of the periphery. No fewer than twenty road blockages were organized by neighbourhood groups (a form of struggle that was unprecedented in the country) in order to demand that the 'Emergency Plan' (which was to give some 50 dollars a month to the poorest families) be applied as quickly as possible in their district. The mobilization of the neighbourhoods has stimulated the government into accelerating implementation of this struggle against poverty, which is rather similar to those that have been launched in Argentina and Brazil.

In sum, the Uruguayan social movement is in the process of adapting to this completely new political context in which power is in the hands of forces that have taken up the demands of the movements. This situation provides the social actors with new opportunities, but it also reveals its limits. In fact, while the trade unions are being strengthened and there is a stronger presence of the poorest people, the unemployed and those who have been marginalized, there is a real risk of the movements becoming subordinated to governmental action. This became clear recently in the conflict between Uruguay and Argentina about the installation of two cellulose factories (see also Chapter 6). In the name of defending employment and supported by a majority of the population, the trade unions joined with the government and the multinational corporations in rejecting the Argentinian ecologists in a climate of national unity that promotes the continuation of the neoliberal model.

Mauricio Archila

9
Democratizing 'democracy' in Colombia

'The country has to choose whether to strengthen "democratic security" or opt for disguised communism that will hand the country over to the FARC.' [1]

Álvaro Uribe Vélez

These words by the candidate for re-election to the presidency clearly show the polarization that Colombia is experiencing. By anachronistically conjuring up the Cold War, Álvaro Uribe Vélez is dividing the country into two: those who agree with his Democratic Security policy and those who are opposed to it, whom he accuses of not only being 'disguised communists', but of delivering the country to the most important guerrilla movement still active in Latin America. Let us look at the context in order to understand the struggles of the dominated sectors of the Colombian population to 'democratize the democracy'.

Colombia has been known for having one of the most stable democracies of the subcontinent which, while it has not undergone the dictatorships that other countries have suffered, is not very 'inclusive'. There has been considerable progress in terms of civil, political, social and cultural rights, which were consecrated in the 1991 constitution, but they are threatened by the new right in power. The present government has proved to be strongly authoritarian, which not only tends to eliminate the opposition but to 'de-institutionalize' democracy, relying on the charisma of the president. His policy of Democratic Security is more concerned with security than with democracy and, apart from a slight reduction in violence and a greater presence of the police, there has been no substantial decrease in human rights violations.

Another characteristic of the country has been its macro-economic stability, which has also been affected by the rupture in its traditional gradualism, following the opening, 'towards the interior', in recent decades. Neoliberalism has diminished the social role of the State to the point that public expenditure in this field has gone from 40 per cent of GDP in the 1980s to the current 12 per cent. Flexibility of the labour force has resulted in unemployment, which reached 20 per cent in 2000 but now stands at 13 per cent.

The last typical aspect of Colombia is the persistence of armed conflict. Uribe Vélez denies its political nature, reducing it simplistically to a manifestation of global terrorism. The presence of so many actors – the paramilitary right, the drug traffickers, the guerrillas and the State's armed forces – each having its own territory, has exacerbated the conflict to the point of creating a profound humanitarian crisis. Although the murder rate has gone down from the mid-nineties, it is still very high: 66 per 100,000 inhabitants, of which 20 per cent is caused by political violence.

Internal displacement is dramatic, too, affecting almost 10 per cent of the population. The present government's solution is to defeat illegal actors by military means in order to force them to negotiate. This policy has not been successful as regards the guerrillas, who have retreated but are far from being defeated. As for the paramilitary right, there have been negotiations which are resulting in 30,000 of them being demobilized. Few will be brought to trial and, if they are, they will receive very light sentences. The whole process is a grim pantomime because, apart from the fact that there will be no justice, truth or reparations, the paramilitaries' structures remain intact and not all of them have been demobilized. Many have not given in their arms, and the politicians, businessmen and military who supported them have not been touched.

Despite this desperate situation, the social actors in Colombia are not resigned. On the contrary, they are struggling to broaden their citizenship, which is precarious. According to the CINEP [2] data bank on social struggle, the number of social protests that have taken place since the re-election of the current president in 2005 has surpassed the historic average established in 1975. Less than six months after the end of Uribe Vélez's first mandate, the trend had been maintained: between October 2005 and March 2006, 202 collective actions were recorded. The urban population, the waged workers and the students have been responsible for three-quarters of the protests in this period, followed far behind by independent workers, peasants, ethnic groups and finally by businessmen, women and prisoners.

During those six months, as happened in the four years of Uribe's first mandate, governmental policies, the violation of basic human rights and the lack of respect for agreements and laws have constituted the causes for 56.8 per cent of all the social struggles. Social services, land and housing, public services and environmental problems – linked to housing and decent living conditions – represent 29 per cent of the demands. The tendency does not mean that Colombia has found solutions for the material problems of poverty and inequity, but that the armed conflict demands that priority be given to respect for life and constitutional guarantees.

In fact, criticism about neoliberal globalization coincides with opposition to official policies and particularly the negotiation of the free trade treaty. As far as the population is concerned, this problematic is connected with the re-election of the president – so much so that the two subjects are often confused. The peasant organizations, who are pessimistic about the effects of the treaty, up until the end of 2005 organized demonstrations which were condemned by the government and repressed by the armed forces. The national day of protest against the free trade treaty and the presidential re-election of 12 October attracted the greatest support over the six-month period (although it was by no means the only protest). Trade unionists, pensioners, students, displaced persons and 'ordinary people' participated in various actions throughout the country. On the same day, peasants and indigenous people denounced the 'Race Day' and condemned the 'new colonialism' of which they considered the free trade treaty to be a manifestation. The effects of world trade on coffee, sugar loaf and apicultural produce also created protests that received huge support from very different social sectors.

The State employees also demonstrated against the cuts in the budget for health, justice and education. The trade-union movement as a whole, although they did not organize many strikes themselves, encouraged mobilization against the government which was incapable of protecting the lives of union leaders and of fulfilling the agreements with the International Labour Organization (ILO) in favour of the national workforce.

All in all, in spite of the president's authoritarianism, the violence and the effects of neoliberalism, the subordinate sectors in Colombia are not resigned, and they are trying actively to build the future. Thus social actors contribute to democracy, pressing for comprehensive citizenship – not only civil and political – whose dimensions are permanent, but also social. They demand socio-economic equality, but with respect for cultural differences. Their action is not limited to protest: they also undertake a wide range of social and political action and new forms of political participation. This is the result of the constitution of a social and political left that is increasingly distancing itself from the insurgency. The victory in the 2003 elections for some local and regional governments – as in Bogota – and the fact that they received support of over 10 per cent of voters in the recent parliamentary elections: these are important steps in consolidating a left-wing bloc, to which should be added representatives from the liberal centre and some conservative personalities.

The polarization that the country is going through certainly overshadows democracy, but it also opens up the possibility of alternatives from the democratic left and the social movements. Only in this way can progress be made towards the utopia of democracy in Colombia.

Notes

1   *El Tiempo,* 6 May 2006, 1-6.
2   Centro de Investigación y Educación Popular, www.cinep.org.co.

II The Near East
and the Maghreb

Sarah Ben Néfissa

10
The reactivation of Arab civil societies and the demand for democracy

There is no doubt that external pressures, particularly that of the United States, to democratize the countries of the Arab region have reactivated civil societies and reinforced their strength *vis-à-vis* their political regimes. And yet the balance-sheet presented at a scientific colloquium in 2000[1] was very equivocal. Compared with the actors and organizations working at the grassroots, mainly the social organizations linked to the Islamist movements, the 'advocacy' actors and organizations suffered from a number of defects. These included: the elusim of their membership; low turnover of members and leaders; lack of internal democracy, and bureaucratization; many internal conflicts and the personalization of power; weak if any communication with their own societies; limitation of their dialogue with the authorities as well as with foreign and international organizations; the negative effects of the organizations serving as providers of new political personnel co-opted by the regimes without going through the election process, thus depriving Arab states of the competence of elites who profit within civil society from 'bargain basement' political roles; and, finally, few striking and concrete results in terms of democracy and the protection of human rights in these countries.

Since September 2001 this verdict is no longer valid. These 'defects' have been found, in the new regional and international situation, to be positive factors that have made it easier for these actors to participate in what could be called 'a globalized debate on democracy in the Arab world'. The characteristics of the animators of Arab civil society, elites at the highest level; their knowledge of today's dominant international language; their practices, experience and know-how in contacts with foreign and international actors; the way they operate in networks; their knowledge about sources of finance, etcetera: all these have facilitated the adaptation of their discourse and ways of operating to the new regional situation and enabled them to talk of an Arab democracy as an alternative to that of defensive Arab regimes, as well as being alternative to those of foreign actors, particularly the Americans.

It can truly be said that these actors from civil society – NGOs, journalists, human rights activists, etcetera – have become genuine political actors in internal Arab affairs and more important than the recognized political parties. If indeed the latter exist, their activities have been blocked by authoritarian regimes and they are victims of the timetables and election deadlines of the internal political scene. They are more or less compromised with the elites in power and conditioned by internal political calculations. In the Arab world today they have left it to civil society to occupy the field in the demand for democracy. The Egyptian experience is exemplary. The main political actors in 2004 and 2005 have not been the recognized political forces but the NGOs, the journalists of the independent press, protest movements like Kifaya, and the judges.

This reactivation has first of all reinforced the relations between the different Arab civil societies. It is based on a general consensus of the activists and civil organizations on the priority of democracy and the need for an in-depth political reform in all their regimes. While being careful to show the difference between their agenda and that of the US government, denouncing its profound ambiguity, but conscious of their weakness within their own societies, Arab civil actors have benefited from the international opprobrium of the Arab regimes to affirm their own positions and, in certain countries, to win a freedom of action that previously did not exist.

The mobilization of people around political reform and democracy has mainly been due to the Arab network of human rights organizations. One can indeed speak of an Egyptian–Moroccan alliance that is responsible for mobilizing Arab civil societies, particularly the Centre for Human Rights in Cairo and the Moroccan Organization for the Protection of Human Rights. These two organizations have grouped around themselves almost all the Arab organizations and activists concerned with human rights, including those from the Gulf. Their main objective has been to voice an alternative Arab discourse to that of the governments and the League of Arab States, not only on political reform but also on key themes in the region: terrorism and Islamism, as well as the most important conflicts like the Palestine question, Iraq, Sudan and, most recently, Lebanon. The second objective of the organizers of the numerous meetings has been to emphasize the real nature of the political reforms promised by Arab political leaders during various summits and meetings to construct the 'Great Middle East'.

It is important to note the way in which this alternative discourse is being expressed. It emerged during the *de facto* participation of Arab human rights organizations in civil forums[2] that took place parallel to the different meetings and summits organized by the League of Arab States. In fact, significantly, the League does not invite NGOs to participate in its activities.[3] It is indeed the activists in the Arab civil forums who invite representatives of the League to participate in their meetings. The League only invites them when forced to do so by pressure from the United Nations,[4] as occurred when a version of the Human Rights Charter[5] was issued in 1994 by the League of Arab States. It was during these meetings and civil forums organized in certain Arab capitals that various common texts and declarations were drawn up.[6] What made them stand out was the desire of those who signed them to distinguish themselves from the archaic nationalistic discourses of the Arab leaders against 'reforms imposed from outside'. It is the Arab regimes, say these documents, that by refusing to listen to the internal demand for reform have permitted foreign intervention. The texts also denounce the cultural, religious and economic pretexts, as well as that of the Palestinian question, put forward by the regimes so as not to undertake change. The regimes are also accused of having encouraged terrorism and religious extremism by their authoritarian attitudes.

These texts demand respect for religious freedom, the rights of women and of 'ethnic' and religious minorities, as well as reform of the status of workers and immigrants, particularly in the Gulf countries.

The reactivation of Arab civil societies has been financed and supported morally by international and regional organizations such as the World Bank, the United Nations, the European Union and various other foreign public organizations, particularly US ones, in the context of 'support to civil societies and promotion of democracy' in the region. The publication of the United Nations Development Programme (UNDP) reports on Human Development in the Arab World[7] gave considerable moral support but it was mainly, although not only, from the European Union that Arab civil societies found material and financial assistance. It would seem that European funds acted as a kind of compensation for the lack of a genuine European alternative policy towards the project for a Great Middle East, which had become the main reference point of international action in the Arab world. There is no doubt that, in this region, US official aid involves a political cost that is hard to bear.

Apart from international and foreign aid, Arab civil societies were also financed and supported by important Western civil organizations, particularly the Euro-Mediterranean Human Rights Network, the International Federation for Human Rights and many other Western foundations and organizations.

However, while Arab civil organizations have developed solid ties with Western and European civil organizations it can hardly be said that there were genuine convergences between them, for various reasons. First, the mobilization and reactivization of Arab civil societies have focused mainly on the question of democracy and politics, and existing contacts are still timid. For the Arab world, it is above all politics that has priority and hence the difficulty of organizing a social forum in the region – apart from the weakness of Arab social movements and trade unions. Also, relations are affected by the broader context of the con-flictual relations between the Arab world and the West. These were already bedevilled by deep misunderstandings well before 11 September 2001, but that event has certainly increased them. One of the stumbling blocks is the Islamist question, both in the Arab countries and in Western and European ones. Similarly, the terrorist attacks, the recent crisis in the *banlieues* in France, the cartoon caricatures of the Prophet, the question of the Near East after the victory of Hamas and finally the 2006 war in the Lebanon have all increased suspicions on both sides. Lastly, and perhaps most important, the effectiveness of 'Arab civil societies' is restricted, in spite of their reactivation over the last few years, because they have no real social basis. This remains the preserve of the Islamist movements, as the recent election results in the Arab world have shown, while the success of Hezbollah in Lebanon against the Israeli army has reinforced this still further.

The Islamist movements in the different countries draw their strength from powerful social organizations but they are not considered 'civil' in dominant international parlance.

Notes

1   The colloquium was entitled 'NGOs and Governance in the Arab World' and was organized in Cairo in March 2000 by Unesco-Most, the Institute for Religion and Democracy, the Centre for Political and Strategic Policies of *Al Ahram* and the Centre d'Etudes et de Documentation Economique, Juridique et Sociale in Cairo.

2   The first civil forum took place in Beirut in 2004 and it issued a declaration: 'A Second Independence: Towards a Political Reform Initiative in the Arab World'.

3   An NGO cannot obtain consultative status to the League of Arab States and hence participate in the work of the permanent Arab Commission on Human Rights unless it is constituted or registered in a member state of the League and unless that state gives its agreement. With a few exceptions, only the organizations close to the powers that be obtain consultative status with the League of Arab States.

4   The UN High Commissioner for Human Rights.

5   By international standards, there were important omissions in this Charter. It guaranteed rights only superficially, gave ample room to restrictions and dispensations to the guaranteed rights and, above all, contained no genuine mechanisms for controlling respect for human rights.

6   See the following declarations: 'A Second Independence: Towards a Political Reform Initiative in the Arab world'; 'Priorities and mechanisms of reform in the Arab world', etc. on the website www.eihrs.org.

7   The three UNDP reports on human development in the Arab world, drawn up by the most important experts in the region, take a very critical view of the social, political and cultural situation in the Arab world. When the reports were published they generated much internal and regional debate.

Azza Khalil

11
Demands grow in Egypt
for social justice and democracy

Neoliberal policies in Egypt have achieved their main goals in the economic sphere by dismantling the public sector and opening wide the scope for the private sector, acting in alliance with its principals and sponsors in the transnational corporations. However, no similar liberalization has been enacted in the political arena, nor was there any loosening of the fetters on public liberties, despite constant claims for real democracy from all constituents of society.

This can be explained by the fact that the new economic elite (the emerging class of businessmen) looks to the local market as simply the place where they can achieve their primitive accumulation – relying on their close, or family, relations with government ministers and the governors of public banks – while they make a sizeable part of their profits as junior allies to some transnational corporation or other. Now that they have their own representatives in government, they no longer look for legitimacy to local class allies, but rather to their transnational sponsors for political support.

It goes without saying that liberties are never granted by any ruling regime without great pressure being exerted by the oppressed masses. In the absence of such popular pressure, some form of liberties may be granted to certain political forces that command a reasonable amount of credibility with the popular masses so as to contain their spontaneous resistance to the pauperization policies implemented by the ruling regime. In Egypt, after decades of authoritarian rule, the situation is such that the ruling elite now has a free choice of political candidates, none of whom have a mass base. Hence there seems to be no need for any democratic concessions, but rather for more virulent repressive measures to counter increasing popular resistance.

External elements are now becoming more important, as the United States is playing an active role in the region, whether in its assumed task of combating Islamic 'terror', through its aggressive wars in Afghanistan and Iraq, or its unlimited support of the Israeli aggression against the Palestinian and Lebanese peoples. As a consequence, the local ruling elite is losing its grip in the face of US intervention in the internal affairs of its own allies under the guise of promoting democracy as the only rampart against the spread of Islamic 'terror'. Such forms of sham democracy were intended to limit the open use of State terror, and to promote some degree of political freedom in order to push forces into power that support the neoliberal policies advocated by the United States. However, these limited forms of democracy resulted in the emergence of Islamic 'terror' in the form of Hamas in Palestine, and the Muslim Brothers in Egypt. Hence, the US reverted once more to encouraging the policy of stark repression by Israel in Palestine, coupled with the criminal, unwarranted aggression against Lebanon. In Egypt, the discourse for so-called democracy was muted in favour of the violent repression of any popular action on behalf of freedom.

At the local level there are also those who reject the old rules of the game, whether they are from the popular masses whose standard of living has dropped to unprecedented levels of pauperization, or from the middle classes and the petty bourgeoisie, who had enjoyed some privileges four decades earlier. Another reason for the rejection was the revolt against the massacres of the Palestinian people by the Israeli aggressors, and the similar aggression by the US against the Iraqi people. Popular rejection is also facilitated by the internet and some Arab media that undermine all attempts at suppressing information (the crimes perpetrated in Palestine or Iraq, or the acts of repression in the streets of Cairo). The internet also plays a positive role in maintaining contact between the forces of popular resistance, as well as with a certain section of the public.

The rising claims for social justice and democracy

By 2003, there was a convergence of many of the currents of opinion calling for change. This was spurred by the US aggression against Iraq –

after Afghanistan – which heralded yet further danger with the proliferation of threats to Syria and Iran. It was clear that concerted action was necessary, and numerous action committees were created, joining the efforts of activists from some legal and illegal parties, independent political activists, human rights NGOs, research centres, artists and literary personalities, as well as professionals active in their associations such as journalists, lawyers, engineers and university staff. Some concentrated their efforts on the demand for democratic change, while others stressed the need for action within their associations. There was also a resurgence of social and class claims, either in organized elitist forms, or in spontaneous sporadic outbursts by the popular masses.

These demands came from various movements such as the 20th March Movement and the Popular Movement for Change as well as the Egyptian Movement for Change (Kifaya), which is the most active movement, spawning splinter movements such as Artists and Writers for Change, Youth and Students for Change, etcetera. Some feminist movements also adopted similar demands, such as Women for Change, Shaefinkom, and so forth.

The main demands for democracy concentrated on the following: amending the Constitution to guarantee the true independence of the legislature and the judiciary *vis-à-vis* the administration, the free election of the president, and the limitation of his prerogatives. In this connection, opposition to imposing the president's son as heir apparent to the presidency also figured prominently on the agenda. Such a constitutional amendment was very timely as the presidential tenure was due to end in 2005, and a change of rules for re-election was indicated.

At the beginning of 2005, an amendment of article 76 of the Constitution was enacted in such a manner that general elections for the presidency were allowed, but with prohibitive conditions for the candidates. Political activists took to the streets in opposition to this amendment and were met with the most violent repression. The election process was boycotted by many activists, who considered it a farce, and indeed the results showed the effects of open intervention by the administration. Later in the year, parliamentary elections were held, and in these many political activists took part, either in the campaign itself, or as monitors of the process. Again the results showed the usual heavy hand of the administration, so that many candidates of the opposition parties – despite their popularity in their constituencies – were ousted by flagrant fraud.

One side effect of such intervention was the revolt of many of the judiciary, who had been put in charge of the election process, but who were outflanked by police action. They were vehemently opposed to this abuse of their authority and linked it with their legitimate demand for true independence of the judiciary. All groups active for political change expressed their solidarity with the judiciary, in actions which continued for some time into 2006. Repression against members of the judiciary was restrained, the full brunt of the police action falling on the supporting activists. In the end a sort of compromise was reached, as the authorities were apprehensive that this conflict would spread to other professional categories, who had even more serious grievances than the judiciary. In the meantime, 20 per cent of the parliamentary seats were won by members of the outlawed Muslim Brotherhood who had circumvented all the government's obstacles. This gave credence to the regime's contention that the only alternative to its rule was Muslim terror.

Some human rights NGOs were active in defending those activists who had been assaulted by the police, issuing statements condemning the repressive police action, and publicizing such statements abroad and through the international media. Some also went to the courts accusing the ministry of the interior of committing atrocities. The web was widely used for such publicity, and many bloggers were active in this respect, spreading their protests over the internet, as well as calls for democratic and social demands. This activity in cyberspace was accompanied with parallel action in the street, including both vocal and silent demonstrations, night vigils in black apparel, as well as publicizing all such actions in the press and in mass meetings, with banners and stickers, etcetera. At times the authorities allowed such demonstrations to show the degree of 'democracy' permitted, but whenever the demonstrations were massive enough, or gained more popular support, they would immediately resort to repressive measures.

Workers and peasants, the main victims of neoliberalism

Workers and peasants are the classes most adversely affected by neoliberal economic policies. Privatization has meant lay-offs for almost a third of the work force in the public sector factories so far privatized – more than half of their total number – and the pace is increasing. The meagre compensation money workers received was soon swallowed up by galloping inflation, which affects the wages of all remaining public sector workers, as well as those of the private sector. In the absence of legitimate trade-union action in defence of their living standards, workers more often resort to various forms of strikes and industrial action, although this is still criminalized under present laws. Strike action took place in many of the privatized companies such as Qaliub Spinning, Telemisr and Delta Spinning and Weaving. There were also industrial actions in Suez at Mechanized Loading and Unloading and Ideal, while there were numerous strike actions and protests in private sector companies such as Oramisr and Capri. In most of these cases, the reason for action was the reduction of wages, or failure to pay them when due. Often compromises were reached, but they never fully met the workers' legitimate demands.

To tackle these deteriorating conditions, many NGOs have been trying to help workers defend their living standards and their trade-union rights. These NGOs include the Coordination Committee for the Defence of Workers' Rights, the National Committee for the Defence of Workers, Workers for Change and the Committee for Workers' Consciousness in Mehalla. They all attempt to defend the cause of the working class by publicizing workers' action, using legal means to defend those rights. They also defend workers' rights to election within their trade unions without intervention from the administration. However, most of these bodies are elitist in composition, and have failed to establish stable organic relationships with the working class.

The plight of the peasants may be even worse. Under the amended law on land tenure, landlords have the right to evict their tenants and raise rents as high as the free market allows. There have been many conflicts because of protests against evictions in Sarando, Bhoot, Kamsheesh and other villages. In each case, the police used violence against the protesters and all the supporting activists, sending them to court for 'disturbing public order'.

Workers and peasants will not be the only victims of the government's recent steps towards privatizing the public health security system, as well as other public services such as higher education. The government also aims at taking over the huge social security fund which is in essence the capital accumulated over fifty years from the contributions of workers and employers to pay for their old age pensions. So the government is confiscating private capital, thus reversing its neoliberal trend! To counter all these attempts, many organizations have been formed by activists, such as the Committee for the Defence of Social Security, the Committee for the Defence of Citizens' Rights, the Popular Committee for the Defence of the Consumer, and the Union of the Unemployed. These committees resort to legal action, and publicity through newspapers and the internet. However, with the exception of the Committee for the Defence of Social Security, they have not succeeded in mobilizing the masses on a large scale.

Activists within and outside the professional associations

Groups of activists were formed within the main professional associations, aiming at revitalizing these bodies, and helping them to play their proper role in defence of their members' interests, and in upholding national goals. This activism has affected the judges, as well as the associations for engineers, the medical profession, lawyers and journalists – the latter two being particularly active. Other groups were formed to revitalize action such as the Democratic Lawyers, the Democratic Engineers, the Engineers for Change, the Engineers Against Sequestration, the 9th of March Movement for the Independence of the Universities, Students for Change, and Revolutionary Students. These bodies attracted members of very different political views, but sometimes they became arenas for political strife, even though their primary aim was to liberate their organizations from tutelage to the government and its ruling party.

Other groups outside any organizations have spontaneously resorted to action in defence of their rights. Examples have been the work-to-rule of the air traffic controllers, the strike of doctors at Zagazig hospital, the protest of lawyers in Port Said and Cairo against police aggression against one of their colleagues, the strike of school principals in Minieh governorate, and the school workers in Sinai. One such action was that of four workers in the Public Emergency Service in Cairo in August 2005, who climbed on to the radio mast and threatened to commit suicide unless their authoritarian director was removed, and their claim granted. All these actions have been motivated by economic grievances and have no political linkages, but they are widespread throughout the country and sometimes display a high degree of militancy.

Despite all these claims for democracy, none of the main freedoms, such as freedom of political and trade-union action, freedom of expression and the free transfer of power, have been secured. The only freedom left to the forces calling for change is that of shouting out loud (under certain conditions), which helps reduce public tension and acts as a safety valve against revolution. The reason for such an assessment is the elitist nature of most of these movements for change, and the absence of organic ties with the popular masses, which are the real force to achieve change.

However, the recent tendency of the regime to restrict its reaction to popular claims for change to violent repression, while enforcing a false cover-up by means of law and order, shows that the safety valve is failing. In contrast, more popular groups are gaining courage, and attempting to follow the example of the Movements for Change, resorting to positive action in pursuit of their claims. Indeed, it is to be hoped that more integration of these two separate currents will take place in the near future, as consciousness of the need for such integration grows, and eventually materializes.

Abdel Nasser Djabi

12
Algeria: From social regimentation to new popular movements

In recent times there have been a number of unorganized contestation movements in Algeria. However, they are not very effective, they are more or less violent, and above all they have no political perspective. Almost every day for years now, in the northern towns as well as those in the extreme South, dozens of popular 'uprisings' are taking place in similar ways, with the same demands almost everywhere: for drinking water, social housing, jobs, etcetera. Faced with these 'uprisings', the administration, the political society and the State are acting as spectators, allowing the situation to deteriorate from day to day. For those involved in these movements, this 'refusal to listen' is all the more incomprehensible in that the financial situation continues to improve and terrorist actions have diminished in intensity. Between the two protagonists, the State on the one hand, and these unorganized contestation movements on the other, civil society, the trade unions and the parties appear paralysed. They do not seem to possess the analytical capacity to understand this continual social ferment and they therefore have no clear strategies of action.

This situation can largely be explained by Boumédienne's original national project that required the regimentation of the social, the worker and the youth forces. All these have been deprived of autonomous political expression in spite of the fact that they supported the project (albeit with a more or less critical stance). This has not promoted the development of democratic collective action as a means of defending common interests. And it is responsible for the paradox that the forces less inclined to defend democracy and pluralism have benefited more than those who have long been struggling for the democratization of the country.

First there was the trade-union and workers' movement

Since the end of the 1960s, the workplace has seen many contestation movements. Sometimes they took the form of workers' strikes[1] and other times they took on less collective forms. These reflected fairly accurately the power relationships between the embryonic Algerian workers' movement and the new social forces in power since independence. This was indeed the most flourishing phase in the history of those forces. It is not surprising that, until the end of the 1970s, most of the movements that were making demands were in the private (national and foreign) sectors, where trade-union experiences had put down their roots during the colonial occupation. These strikes and contestation movements rarely lasted very long. Their main motivation could be described as 'economistic' – the improvement of working conditions.

With the development of the public sector, with its huge labour force, modern technology, and qualitatively different management of human resources, the workers in the private sector were forced to cede their role as principal actors to the workers in the State sector. Public investment had brought its returns in the form of an industrial structure that facilitated the formation of a new class of workers. Before its later defeat, this workers' movement had known what might be called an 'era of strength and hope', in other words an 'offensive' period. Its demands were varied and strikes became radicalized. They lasted longer and more workers participated in them, while the organization of the public economy in large enterprises with units distributed in several regions turned them into 'national strikes'. They acquired a capacity to negotiate, a sign that the workers' movement and its demands had become more mature.[2]

The working world, composed of workers and trade unions, then entered into a defensive phase, which was to last for more than a decade. In fact, it coincided with the crisis of the development model adopted by the State after independence. This involution was the direct result of the recession that hit the economy and the lack of productive public investment from the early 1980s. As a consequence, a number of factories and production units were closed and there were massive lay-offs. Unemployment and the informal economy expanded. The situation became all the more serious in that the political tendencies known for their unfailing support of the workers' movement (the left, the modernizing nationalists, etcetera) suffered from an ideological impasse. Thus religious tendencies began to return to the forefront of the political field: conservative and neoliberal as they were, they knew nothing of the working world – when, indeed, they were not openly hostile to it.

Trade-union pluralism was recognized in 1990 at a time when the workers' movement was still in its defensive phrase, but it did not help the workers to extract themselves from it. The civil servants (teachers, health professionals and administrators) rapidly formed their own autonomous unions, which were independent of the General Union of Algerian Workers (UGTA), whose representativity continued to decline. Some 'autonomous unions' were established under direct ideological influences such as radical Islamism. Even though they are officially recognized by the administration and in spite of the genuine representativity of some of them, the autonomous unions still have not succeeded, after more than a decade of existence, in getting the State to recognize their right to participate in national-level social negotiations. These always take place with the participation of the three parties: the government, the business leaders and the UGTA.

The student movement: from elitism to the democratization of schooling

The increase in the number of students and the expansion of the university network did not help the student movement, which has had to give up much of its dynamism and autonomy. Up to the early 1970s the movement was concentrated in a few large towns and was considered one of the most influential currents in the social movement. It raised a number of political questions, both national and international, and its views were not necessarily those of the authorities. But it has lost, as well as its elitist character, its political and organizational autonomy. It was given a pounding by the regime shortly after the trade-union movement suffered the same fate, between the end of the 1960s and the beginning of the 1970s.

From the end of the 1970s, the student movement became divided culturally and politically. The democraticization of schooling enabled children from rural popular and middle classes to attend university, just at a time when the whole question of Arabization had become acute. This was a crucial issue in that it had a 'cultural' effect on the student movement. The beginning of the Arabization process coincided with the first signs that the economical development model adopted since independence was losing steam, and this setback provided opportunities for certain opposition forces like Berberism and Islamism. Thus the official discourse on the correct socio-economic options that had been followed since 1962 became increasingly uncertain. For the first time, Algeria began to experience the graduate unemployment phenomenon. The university system had ceased to play its role in socially promoting the children from the popular classes.

The student movement lost much of its influence on the political scene after the recognition of multipartyism and trade-union pluralism. The arena for political confrontation moved far away from the university. The new popular social movements have not depended much on support from the student movement, even after it was taken over by the Salafi Islamist tendency. After that takeover, the student movement began to maintain links with the social movement, but clearly following it, in contrast to the long period when it was in the avant-garde.

The women's movement: emancipation through 'development'

The dominant official discourse after independence served to camouflage, under an apparent 'modernism', a basic conservatism concerning the rights of women. On this issue, an almost total ideological consensus between influential circles of the regime and the semi-legal opposition took shape. Because of this consensus, Algerian women were not able to raise their specific problems separately from the general problems of society. It made the birth of an important women's movement difficult during this period of Algerian history.

While after independence the schooling of girl children continued apace,[3] socially dominant conservative values for a long time thwarted the desire of women to become part of the world of work.[4] But Algeria's economic crisis, particularly in the 1990s, forced families to reduce the conditionalities for women to go to work outside the household. It is now quite commonplace to see women occupying low-skilled jobs in the informal economy which has flourished following the liberal changes in the overall economy. The growing presence of women in the labour market has, however, negative aspects. They are often deprived of the legal protection that the official labour market provides, which makes their social status still more precarious.

Algerian women have finally obtained a semi-recognition of the legitimacy of their demands. This is in contrast with past times when, within those tendencies in favour of women's emancipation, they were denied the right to organize themselves independently. The women's movement has not, however, been able to benefit greatly from political pluralism to build up its influence within society. It remains fundamentally elitist, in spite of the facts that its organizational forms have diversified and many women have been able to emerge. Some have had important positions – ministers, parliamentarians, party leaders. But women's organizations have not succeeded in developing their influence in the student world, despite their increasing numbers, or in the female professional milieu which is theoretically more disposed to share their ideas. As for the rural world, it has been totally overlooked by this movement which has never left the large towns, particularly the capital, where it first appeared.

The new social movements

The religious movements

The new social movements have brought new actors into the political arena: young people from the towns and the popular quarters. They rejected their living conditions in a new, ambiguous political language, often referring to their Islamic religious inheritance. Breaking with the discourse of the traditional social movements (workers, unions, students), they invented a new language of demands, which was extremely powerful, and it soon became an effective way of mobilizing people – a mobilization that the middle classes had failed to organize. The latter were mostly francophone and provided the traditional social movements with most of their members.

A characteristic of these new popular social movements is their all-embracing discourse, in which it is difficult to distinguish the moral from the religious, or the collective from the private, for they are all aggregated into the same indissoluble body. Another characteristic is their radicalism, which gives them a ready audience among the popular classes. This accounts for the way young people have been able to dominate mass action with an unprecedented enthusiasm. Before being taken over by the Salafi tendency, these movements concentrated on various aspects of living conditions (housing, work, education). They soon occupied social spaces other than the factory or the university, which had been fiefs of the traditional social movements. They occupied the stadiums and the popular quarters on the periphery of the important towns, before extending their influence to the mosques. And they brought with them new forms of religiosity but above all a highly politicized oppositional discourse.

It has never been possible for the 'nationalist' tendencies, with the memory of their past management of the country, to recruit these popular social movements, which could be considered crude when they started out. Nor could they be taken in hand by the different left-wing tendencies, elitist and francophone, who come from the urban middle classes. At the beginning the youth were not even recruited by the religious tendencies. The Salafi tendency, which was hegemonic and well entrenched in the popular classes, referred to them as common rabble, considering their religious purity too questionable to be worthy of support. But when these new movements reached their peak, during the events of October 1988, they made a historic decision to join the radical religious tendency represented by the Salafi tendency of the Islamic Salvation Front (FIS).

By adopting the new social movements, the radical religious tendency provided their discourse with an all-embracing character, bringing together the sacred and the profane. Above all, they gave them new perspectives, moral and religious, which the new social movements had lacked, as they were originally 'modern' movements born of the daily distress of most of the urban population, especially the youth. The radical religious tendency led these contestatory movements into violent confrontation, not only with the State and its various apparatuses, but also with the other social forces that had alienated them with their exclusivist discourse and practices. As a result violence broke out which fed a blind terrorism whose main victims came from the popular classes.

The cultural movements

A chronological history of the Algerian social movements would certainly refer to the Berber cultural movement (MCB), which existed before the religiously oriented popular social movements arrived on the scene. In spite of all the restrictions imposed by the regime on the country and the prestige acquired by the official national model, the culturalist Berber tendency succeeding in making itself felt – if only partially – through some of the opposition parties like the FFS (the Front of Socialist Forces) and the RCD (the Union for Culture and Democracy) and even, from time to time, through the traditional social movements (workers, students, etcetera).

Emigration to France, which has traditionally been strong, together with education, have profoundly changed Kabyle society, which is rural and conservative. These two developments have influenced the social movements in this region which, since the revolt of April 1980 (commonly known as the Berber Spring), have always been distinguished for the excellence of their cadres and for the participation of the elites in their action. In Kabylia the cultural social movements have always been inter-class movements, mobilizing the workers and peasants as well as shopkeepers, students and businessmen. The FFS and the RCD have sometimes succeeded in linking the specific preoccupations of the region to other more 'national' questions (like the elections, Islamist terrorism, the security situation). Thus the cultural social movements have fitted into a broader ideological movement, marked by the strong presence of the urban middle classes, as well as women, who call for democracy, human rights, and, sometimes, the struggle for secularism.

The violent uprisings that shook Kabylia in 2001 and 2002 were a clear sign of the crisis, if not the defeat of the popular cultural movement. It has lost many of its former characteristics, such as pacifism and its organizational framework. During the riots it did not express itself through the traditional context of parties (FFS and RCD), trade unions or associations, but in the new movements of the Arches and the neighbourhood committees. The old generation of leaders was replaced by another, more attached to the local identity but also far more radical. This radicalism was shown in the demands for the closing of the gendarmerie brigades, as well as their units in the countryside who were trying to prevent the holding of legislative and local elections in the region in 2002.

The convulsions and insecurity that Kabylia has undergone over the past five years have been exacerbated by the economic and social problems that have continued to accumulate for more than a decade in this region. Under the combined effect of the internal economic crisis and the increasingly draconian control of European frontiers, the traditional migratory flows – towards France and the rest of the country – have dried up, which has brought about a radical change in the demographic structure of the region. This tendency to return to the 'local', towards the 'cultural, quasi ethnic' has benefited from the discreet encouragement of the State, particularly since the end of the 1990s. It is happening at a moment when the national State itself, its institutions, its leading elites and its discourse are all undergoing a profound crisis.

Notes

1   See my book *Algeria in Movement: a Socio-political Study of the Workers' Strike Movements*, Dar El Hikma, Algiers, 1999 (in Arabic).

2   Nevertheless, in spite of this maturity, the movement failed to build up alliances, both within and outside the working world, even with the forces that were objectively close to them, such as the management cadres of the public sector and certain categories of qualified and administrative employees, towards whom many of the workers had an exclusionary attitude, motivated by a 'worker' mentality that coloured many trade-union practices. Thus the movement did not succeed in forming an effective social bloc in the working world. This would have certainly reinforced their position when they were later in a defensive phase.

3   Girls formed 60 per cent of some 500,000 candidates for the *baccalauréat* examination in 2006.

4   Only highly qualified work for women was permitted.

Fatiha Dazi-Héni

13
Social awakening in the Arabian Peninsula: the oil monarchies adapt

Regional events in the Arab Peninsula (Arabia) in the 1990s – the war for the liberation of Kuwait in 1991 and a period of economic austerity due to the low cost of oil (about 11 to 13 dollars a barrel until the beginning of 1998) – stirred up the collective conscience of both regimes and societies. For both, nothing would be the same any more: the time was gone when these welfare states used to buy social peace by redistributing the revenue from oil. Rather than confining ourselves to the classic approach emphasizing the authoritarian character of the six monarchies of the Arab Peninsula, or the conservative tribal and religious reality that dominates these societies, it is instructive to study the dynamics set in motion by these six authoritarian regimes to adapt themselves to the increasing demands from their societies (Dazi-Héni 2006).

How did these societies succeed in forcing the reigning dynasties to renegotiate social pacts that had remained unchanged since the tribal fiefdoms set themselves up as hereditary dynasties? Over the last decade there have been various processes in the different monarchies of the region, through which power has been renegotiated by the ruling families in order to integrate a local elite that had been excluded from politics and that now tends to use its weight to impose new options in economic policies.

The Arabian territories, transformed into sovereign national lands at the beginning of the twentieth century, were first dominated by the old tribal chiefs. These became hereditary dynasties through protection treaties guaranteed by the British empire (Zahlan 1998). The oil rent, of which the usufruct and redistribution were taken over by the reigning families, helped to reinforce the authoritarian character of these *rentier* countries that had become royal powers, thanks to colonization. The analyses of the State and societies of this region by the Kuwaiti sociologist Khaldun al-Naqeeb are a major reference work in this regard (1990). Moreover, he shows how this institutional corporatism stifled all the attempts of civil society at autonomy. It is at the origin of the lack of democracy[1] that still today prevails in the region, according to this writer, who is considered an authority in the Arab and international academic world.

Calls for democratization and economic liberalization

I am particularly concerned here with the ways whereby civil society affirms itself, going beyond the political study that delves into the dense literature dedicated to authoritarianism, particularly as concerns the states of the Middle East and *a fortiori* the pyramidal structure of the dynastic states of the Arab Peninsula. The second oil shock, which occurred between 1986 and 1988, and the geopolitical atmosphere of the 1990s, strongly influenced the decision of the monarchs to adapt to the changes being demanded by their young people (below 25 years) who constitute on average nearly 70 per cent of the national population of these countries. During the 1990s, Arab society, which until then had been totally controlled by the State, gradually became made up of social actors in their own right. The autocratic regimes in Saudi Arabia, Oman, Qatar, United Arab Emirates, Kuwait and Bahrain were forced to react to this new development, albeit each in its own way.

Calls for democratization and more transparent governance were increasingly insistent after the Kuwait war, not only in Kuwait itself, but also in Saudi Arabia, Bahrain and, to a lesser extent, Oman. In contrast, in Qatar and the United Arab Emirates (UAE), particularly Dubai, it was the princes of the new generation who took the initiative of making important changes, but apart from these two cases, socio-demographic developments were the most effective levers in obliging the authoritarian regimes of the Arab Peninsula to adapt themselves to the new demands and to proceed with economic liberalization.

There are clear signs that an elite of social actors, up until then excluded from decision-making circles, began to make itself felt. Many of them came from the middle classes, 'rentier children', having profited from the largesse of the policies to redistribute revenues from oil income. They were at the heart of the negotiations of new social pacts that have been developing since the end of the 1990s in Saudi Arabia and, though to a lesser extent, in Oman, but also in Qatar and Dubai. Bahrain and Kuwait, whose political development has been in the avant-garde in the region, had integrated their graduate elites from the middle classes from 1970 (Bahrain) and 1980 (Kuwait).

The classic forms of rule that had been used by the most conservative dynastic regimes of the peninsula became untenable. The new period saw the current changes that will have decisive repercussions on the capacity of these monarchical regimes to perpetuate themselves in future.[2] In the period after the Kuwait war, they were forced to take structural adjustment measures, both to respond to strong socio-demographic pressures, as well as to make their economies more attractive to foreign capital and investment. It is clear that the economic crisis that followed the steep depreciation in oil prices from 1987 made these regimes, a few years later, reconsider their modes of functioning. The speech of the former heir to the throne, Crown Prince Abd Allah, on 18 May 1998, when he spoke of the end of the welfare state in Saudi Arabia, can be interpreted in this light.[3]

To a greater or lesser degree, the regimes are confronted with demographic constraints and varying levels of reserves of hydrocarbons as well as political cohesion, all of which condition the strength of their consensus. These structural differences impact on the capacity and will of the leaders to make changes. To abandon welfare policies and the assistance to which their peoples are accustomed means that the State will no longer be the main employer and creator of new jobs for nationals. The private sector is being encouraged to share the burden that was previously borne by the State alone. These are challenges that the monarchical regimes of Arabia have to tackle.

Adaptation of the dynastic regimes

This transition does not involve the same level of risks in each of the six countries studied: the pattern is not uniform. Their rulers are nevertheless all confronted by the need to establish new social pacts, particularly by making an economic transition through adopting liberalization measures, such as privatization. It means abandoning the sponsor system, known as *kafila*,[4] which prevented foreign companies from fully owning property until the beginning of the present decade.

The Cooperation Council for the Arab States of the Gulf[5] has been something of a failure in the political and security fields, but progress has been made in economic integration: there is free circulation and movement of persons, ownership of property, and common investment institutions, and there will be a common currency as from 2010. The restructuring of the economic organization marks a new stage in the history of the monarchical regimes for it mainly consists in contracting other types of alliances, without however upsetting the traditional coalitions.

This process is particularly noticeable in Dubai, where the new emir has taken over his father's modernizing vision for the development of the city. Sheikh Muhammad Bin Râshid Al Maktûm, Emir of Dubai and Prime Minister of the United Arab Emirates (UAE), has succeeded in carrying out his city-world project through co-opting local technocrats trained in Singapore and the United States, who have become the spearhead for the changes and for the success of the Dubai model. Some emphasize the autocratic nature of such a method and they are not wrong, but the interest of the example lies in quite another field. For these technocrats now occupy a preponderant place in the new Dubai. Moreover, the authoritarian mechanism of forming clients out of a new elite linked to the visionary project of a political leader is not peculiar to Dubai.

The Saudi case is also fascinating to study in this context of the dynamics of change. A phase of negotiation is at present under way which the Al Saoud regime, under the leadership of King Abd Allah, at that time Regent, started in 1998. It was reactivated by the events of 11 September 2001, although this was more in the nature of an acceleration of the process, rather than triggering mechanisms of national dialogue and renegotiation of the social pact. Nevertheless, the geopolitical context, with the United States pressurizing the kingdom to renounce its Wahabi ideology, reinforces resistance to change, even if the changes form part of the process of transformation and do not necessarily lead to major crises.

Far more so than after the Kuwait war in 1991, after 11 September

2001 civil societies emerged that reflected the views of most nationals who desired to discuss, on an equal basis with their leaders, crucial questions of national interest (security, public expenditure or social problems such as youth unemployment). The regimes were most attentive to this development, as was also the United States, although for different reasons. It is true that the desire for change has not been equally intense in all countries, just as the parameters for negotiations to find a new *modus vivendi* between the regimes and societies are not the same. It is all too common to refer to this group of states as one historical ensemble, culturally, economically and politically. But although there are similarities, this apparent uniformity masks complex and diversified experiences.

Thus it will be much more difficult for the Al Saoud dynasty to find an ideal solution for a new social contract, also because the royal family, which is very numerous and divided into rival clans, will have to decide by consensus. This is now a constraint that for the time being confronts Bahrain, Qatar, Dubai, Oman and Abu Dhabi. The death of the patriarch assures continuity, with the accession of Sheikh Khalîfa as Emir of Abu Dhabi and President of the UAE Federation. However, this continuity does not prevent continued strong competition from the rival Al Nahyâ clans. Recently, the Kuwaiti parliament spectacularly removed Sheikh Sa'ad, the impotent heir apparent to Emir Jaber, who died on 15 January 2006, and unanimously supported the number three of the regime, Sheikh Sabah Al Ahma, who became Emir in conformity with the Kuwaiti constitution.

The authoritarian ruling tactics that preserved the old alliances and governed according to a corporatist strategy will increasingly give place to bargaining and negotiation in order to integrate other social groups (technocrats, new businessmen) who will co-exist with the royal families, if not replace the old allied elites in the future.

Notes

1 On this point, see also Gh. Salamé (1991), *Sur la causalité d'un manque: pourquoi le monde arabe n'est-il donc pas démocratique?*
2 For a study of the historical and political developments in the monarchical regimes of the Arab Peninsula and their capacity to perpetuate themselves, see

M. Herb (1999), *All in the Family: Absolutism, Evolution and Democratic Prospects in the Middle Eastern Monarchies*.

3   Extracts of this speech were published on 20 May 1998 in the daily newspaper *al-Watân*, which was launched that year by Prince Khâlid Al Faysal Al Saoud (governor of the province of 'Asir and brother of Saoud Al Faysal, Minister of Foreign Affairs).

4   This regulatory principle prevents foreign investors from possessing a majority of the shares in one company and keeps strict control over the rights of distribution. Thus it guarantees local elites a monopoly over commercial activities, including a sector as strategic and flourishing as national defence. The principle still prevails in the non-duty-free zones, but with five of the six countries adhering to the GCC (see note 5) and the forthcoming adhesion of Saudi Arabia to this multilateral trade body, the principle is destined to disappear definitively.

5   The Gulf Cooperation Council (GCC) was adopted by the six monarchies of the Arab Peninsula and renamed the Cooperation Council for the Arab States of the Gulf in 1990. However the acronym GCC continues to be used.

Kamal Lahbib

14
Morocco: Hopes and fears and 'sit-in wars'

It is difficult to foresee how this current period in Morocco is going to turn out, with all the struggles being waged by various forces in society. Unrest persists, full of ambivalence and paradoxes, and it is endangering the gains from the transition to democracy. This is all exacerbated by the spectre of terrorism, by the corruption that is rotting the political system and discrediting political action and institutions, and by the incapacity to reduce social disparities and injustices and establish policies to establish accountability.

Economic globalization and the reduction of the role of the State that goes with it, particularly in public services, are creating structural upheavals that call into question the very framework in which people organize their lives. The international conjuncture aggravates the situation further. The war in Iraq, the Israeli invasion and violence in Lebanon and Gaza, the setback to the Barcelona process that promised a zone of shared wealth and stability, the signing of a free trade agreement with the United States, the gendarme role that the European Union wants to play in Morocco, confronted with an emigration that is increasingly tragic and suicidal: all these have had a direct impact on the social and political scene in Morocco, in spite of measures taken by the State to eradicate poverty, the billion euros of the compensation fund for maintaining the prices of basic necessities, and an inflation rate of only 2 per cent, even if there has been an explosion in energy bills.

The many mobilizations and sit-ins

The collective reactions to these new conditions have varied. They all started with massive urban demonstrations attacking the cost of living. The new social movements are distinguishable from the old ones by their actors and by their concrete forms of action. Although they are not spontaneous, they are not the tools of the parties and trade unions. They have helped to bring different forms of action under the lenses of the media projectors: new ways of occupying streets, petitions, complaints, recourse to justice, the use of the internet, recourse to spectacular forms of action attracting media attention, like the unemployed graduates (whose sit-ins are part of the décor of the capital), who have also tried to set fire to themselves, etcetera.

The reasons for these contestations are essentially linked to purchasing power: they include protests against the increase in transport costs, the expense of medical care dispensed by the public hospitals, and the mounting water and electricity bills. Forty-six sit-ins were organized in one week, mobilizing several thousand people throughout the kingdom to protest against the last rise in the cost of basic food items. However, some demonstrations were about insecurity, while still others, encouraged by the National Human Development Initiative,[1] demand social development projects for opening up villages to the outside world. These demonstrations, sit-ins and peaceful marches have affected even remote and hitherto unknown villages: at Oued Zem, Tighza, Mrirt, Itzer, Aghbalou, Boumya, Lakbab, Tata, where 'defence committees' support the inhabitants of all the towns that want to improve their social situation. These far-off areas, which have long been forgotten, relegated to being part of 'useless Morocco', are on the move. Some of them, like the region of Khénifra, have overcome the shock and fear of the atrocities of the 1973 repression.

The struggle to safeguard the environment has also spilled over from the aseptic framework of seminars and been adopted by people mobilized in local associations. It ranges from denouncing the pillage of sand from the beaches by construction companies to protests against the pollution of ground water by factories and municipal rubbish dumps. It also includes a struggle against the emissions of dust created by phosphate mining.

Sit-ins that are political, but also elitist, have been organized by left-wing parties and associations defending human rights against the violence of the State (a 'National network against the excessive aggression of the public authorities against citizens' has been set up), against the free trade agreement with the United States, against the visit of Donald Rumsfeld to Morocco, against the holding of the NATO summit, against the scandalous use of money to buy candidates and the 'grands électeurs' during the last elections to renew a third of the Chamber of Councillors. It is particularly significant that there has been a sit-in on behalf of truth and justice and against impunity, which was held in front of the secret detention centre PF3 (Poste Fixe 3), one of the most important secret detention centres, where many militants fighting for justice and democracy have met their deaths.

The sit-in has become so common that the press talks of the 'the sit-in war' to refer to the struggle between the Islamists and the democratic forces. Sit-ins have also been organized against a weekly for having reproduced the Danish cartoons, and against the Moroccan Human Rights Association for making proposals on behalf of the 'Tindouf sequestered persons' that were considered outrageous. On top of that there was the possible contagion of Kabylia (in Algeria), with the demonstrations organized by the Amazigh associations, the drama of the Sub-Saharans for whom Morocco is a transit place, with its xenophobia and its surprises, the young unemployed, captivated by the mirage of the European eldorado, the revolt by the peoples of the Sahara, the difficult reconciliation with the Rif which has been marginalized for decades, and so forth.

Globalization and the new technologies are responsible for the 'hactivists', the new generation of 'cyber-militants' who participate in the resistance by making virus attacks against US and Israeli sites. A young 18-year-old hacker has just been condemned to two years in prison for having attacked the sites of large US companies. The Team Evil group attacked 850 Israeli sites in June 2006, declaring that 'as long as you kill Palestinians, we shall kill your servers'. The group of e-demonstrators is now very active in the IT combat against the occupation of Palestine by Israel and that of the US army in Iraq. By April 2006 they had already pirated over 7,605 sites, some of them very big ones, like that of the Israeli Institute for Biological Research and McDonalds Israel. This is a new generation which delights in technological performance and is influenced by the Al Jazeera media, who consider that Nasrallah has saved the honour of the Arabs.

Progress of democracy, but increasing social division

All these contestations show that progress has been made in broadening the field of freedom. They also show the profound change in the behaviour of the contestants. We are far from the violent explosions of 1981 and 1984, but we are also far from the systematic and generalized violent reactions of the State. The protest movements are sometimes repressed, sometimes authorized or desired, sometimes tolerated. It is also true that there has been progress in implementing the Moudawana (family code), through the Equity and Reconciliation Body (IER) which, in public hearings on the media has undertaken a genuine collective therapy against fear in the struggle against sexual tourism and corruption and even in the fight against impunity. Urban security groups have been dissolved for having committed violence against citizens, while crooked parliamentarians and those close to the palace have been brought to justice. These are important achievements to be put to the credit of the governments that have come to power since the consensual changeover in 1999.

However, in spite of all these efforts – the governmental actions, the royal initiatives, international and national financial support to civil society – the country has not managed to overcome the social divide. For it has been Morocco's adherence to neoliberalism and the consequent privatization of public services that has aggravated social divisions. The growth proclaimed is useless if it is to end up as 'production fetishism'.[2] The resistance, while it is a legitimate and salutary phenomenon, is symptomatic of a serious social and political crisis. This expression of social discontent cannot be resolved by violence and the security approach of the State, which only stirs up general resentment. The dilemma is common in all the emerging countries in a transition phase: the State is trapped between, on the one hand, the aspirations of the overwhelming majority of the population for a decent standard of living and, on the other hand, the spate of injunctions coming from the international financial institutions.

Behind all these paradoxes is the fundamental question that torments us: how to 'mobilize the grassroots' to bring about significant social change and the institutional change favourable to social development? What forms of militant action should be undertaken in this period of socio-economic restructuring that is going on around the world? What is certain is that without a restructuring of the democratic camp, whose components are weak, divided, ageing and with closed mind-sets, the opening up of the democratic process will benefit the fundamentalists, who will know how to take advantage of democratic principles in order to crush democracy.

Notes

1 Social improvement, a complex and long-term task, cannot come about through one-off measures or spontaneous charity, or through ethical concerns or greater awareness.
2 As Alain Lipietz has emphasized, 'The growth in the well-being of some is created by a decrease in the waste of others'.

Michel Warschawski

15
Israel–Palestine:
A lack of perspective

The war in Lebanon confirmed that there was a very broad political consensus in Israel. Unlike the 1982 war, there was no mass opposition to it, and the few thousand militants who denounced this new bloody adventure were the exception proving the rule. This new consensus, put together by the former Labour prime minister, Ehud Barak, reversed the perceptions of what is called the peace movement. It is no longer the Palestinians who are the victims of the occupation, colonization and military repression, but it is Israel which is in danger of being wiped out, in the context of the clash of civilizations of which Islam is the main actor and the Palestinians the immediate tool.

At the Camp David negotiations in July 2000 Barak succeeded in presenting the real intentions of the Palestinians as being to throw the Jews into the sea. Since then Israel has had to pursue a permanent and preventive war against a danger that is, for some, cynically constructed and, for others, imaginary. The occupation of the West Bank and the Gaza Strip, which has been the object of political debate for almost a quarter of a century and which even led to the assassination of the prime minister in 1995, is no longer seen by moderate Israelis as being the heart of the problem, just as withdrawal from the occupied territories is no longer considered to be the key to peace between Israel and its neighbours. The problem has become that of the very existence of Israel, and the solution – endless war. 'We are a villa in the heart of the jungle', as Ehud Barak himself said, implying that peace was only a trap.

Primitive anti-Islamism

Thus the new consensus believes that Israel has no credible partner and that the Arab world, indeed the Muslim world, is all ready to destroy the Hebrew state, so that it is necessary to shut themselves up (or, rather, shut up the Palestinians) behind a wall and carry out preventive wars. This conception fits in perfectly with the North American strategy of global, endless war, and indeed it was elaborated by the neoconservatives of the two countries from the end of the 1980s. The lack of mass opposition to the war in Lebanon, as also to the campaign of reconquest and terror in the occupied territories, confirms the damage that has been wrought by the deceptive discourse of the Israeli neoconservatives.

And yet, in spite of the consensus and the crushing military superiority of Israel, the Lebanese war was a political fiasco and a military defeat – to such a point that numerous commissions of enquiry have been set up to try and understand this apparent paradox. But do we really need commissions of enquiry to understand this fiasco? With the expectation that an important part of the international community would be for a neutralization of Hezbollah, integrated into the strategy of the permanent war against terrorism, and tainted by the 'clash of civilizations' philosophy and primitive anti-Islamism, the political and military Israeli leaders, sure of their overwhelming military superiority, went off to war without preparation, without clear objectives and without an operational plan.

In Israel, colonial arrogance has long replaced political thinking and military preparation. It came up against the resistance of Hezbollah and the Lebanese people who, contrary to all the Tel Aviv scenarios, supported the resistance against an aggression that attacked the population and infrastructures of Lebanon. It is as simple as that and all commissions of enquiry are quite superfluous.

To that should be added the devastating effects of unbridled neo-liberalism, which encourage the Israeli leaders – including their military chiefs of staff – to be more concerned with lining their own pockets rather than looking after the public interest. Many of them are involved in corruption and embezzlement, and the less cunning of them are actually being brought into the courts. Israel is afflicted by corruption, and this internal rot risks, eventually, doing more harm to the Jewish state than war threats and any return to terrorist attacks.

Internal crises and deteriorating living conditions

It is this internal crisis which, despite the huge gap in power relationships, makes for a common denominator between Israel and the occupied Palestinian territories. For Palestinian society is also undergoing a serious internal crisis which, although it has developed further through the Israeli occupation, cannot be attributed solely to this. In the eyes of the Palestinians, the failure of the PLO was threefold: it did not know how to liberate its people from the Israeli occupation, it was made ridiculous during a negotiation process that rapidly became a charade, and it was incapable of managing with minimum efficiency the problems of daily life of the West Bank and the Gaza Strip, part of its leadership also being tarnished by corruption.

For these three reasons it lost the trust of the public, who have turned to Hamas in a protest vote. No one, including Hamas itself, had foreseen how massive this would turn out. By electing a Hamas government, the Palestinians showed that they had recognized the stalemate of the negotiation process, and they expected a clean-up of public affairs and a relative improvement in their living conditions. But they did not reckon with the international reaction to the – democratic – victory of the Islamists.

Under pressure from Israel and the Bush administration, the international community, including some Arab countries, decided to punish the Palestinian people for having 'voted badly'. Instead of boycotting Israel for its daily and systematic violations of international law and its contempt for the various UN resolutions, it is the Palestinians who are treated to an international boycott, the Gaza Strip having been subjected to an economic blockade that has caused a serious humanitarian crisis.

The dramatic situation of the Palestinian population, particularly in Gaza, and the inability of the Hamas government to improve the living conditions of more than three million people, have encouraged the Fatah hardliners to try to reverse forcibly the democratic choice of the Palestinian voters. The armed confrontations in Gaza during September 2006 revealed that the American–Israeli plans to destabilize the society, if not provoke a civil war, have found their Palestinian counterparts within one of the Fatah tendencies.

Lack of any political perspective and the degradation of living conditions are atomizing Palestinian society as people fall back on their tribal origins, and there is a risk that internal conflicts will multiply. There is also a risk of reinforcing Islamization, as opposed to the Palestinians' original national and secular orientation. The popularity of Ahmadinejad and his ultra-radical discourse is indisputable and, following its success when confronted with the Israeli army, Hezbollah is increasingly seen as the example to follow.

Succeeding Israeli governments have acted as sorcerer's apprentices over the last decade, promoting the denationalization of the conflict as well as giving it a religious dimension. Thus there is the enormous risk of regionalizing the conflict. For the Palestinians, the war in Lebanon constituted an important step towards regionalizing their problem and their struggle. Israel will no doubt regret this, but only when it is too late.

Gülçin Erdi Lelandais

16
Turkey: Alternative world struggles, identity struggles and the centralizing inheritance

Turkey is one of the rare countries in the Middle East where globalization has progressed at a comparable rhythm to that of the West, in all fields. Since 1980, the Turkish economy has made every effort to adapt to and integrate into the world economy, under the leadership of international institutions such as the International Monetary Fund (IMF), the World Bank, the World Trade Organization and the European Union. Within the country the burden of structural adjustment policies has been felt more heavily since the economic crisis linked to the flight of capital in 2001 and the privatization programmes, including those for the large public enterprises.

Among the population this forced-march development has provoked various reactions, linked both to the influence of the international financial institutions and the United States and to the candidature of Turkey to the European Union. Schematically they can be divided into two: one formed around reactionary and nationalistic sentiments, emphasizing national honour in the face of external enemies, while the other interprets the social and political problems of the country in light of globalization and the local struggles in other countries. In 2005 and 2006, there were protests in different towns in Turkey. But this mounting contestation can equally be explained by the arrival to power of the 'moderate Islamic' party, the Justice and Development Party (AKP), and by the important juridical reforms in civil liberties that form part of the process of Turkey's adhesion to the European Union.

Against war and globalization

The social, political and cultural contestation is grouped around three main issues. The first grouping developed just after the events of 11 September 2001 and was subsequently transformed by a broad movement of protest against the hegemonic war of the United States, but also to defend human rights in the countries attacked by the US. At the centre of it is the Küresel Bariş ve Adalet Koalisyonu – BAK (Coalition for Global Peace and Justice). This movement has been involved in a number of events in recent years, for example the campaign for the closing of the American military base at Incirlik (in southern Turkey), anti-war action days organized simultaneously with other countries on 19 March and 24 September 2005, and the last session of the Peoples' Tribunal on Iraq, which was held in Turkey under BAK's auspices.

A second grouping concentrates on the struggle against capitalism, the international financial institutions and the problems created by globalization for workers and peasants. This tendency has launched significant actions against the privatization of public enterprises such as PETKIM (petrochemicals), TEKEL (alcoholic drinks and tobacco) and SEKA (paper), whose privatization and closure led 734 workers and their families into occupying the factory for twenty-two days. At a completely different level there was an action against the Asian Development Bank which held its thirty-eighth conference from 4 to 6 May 2005 in Istanbul.

While these struggles were in the main organized by trade unions, particularly KESK and DISK and the professional chambers of engineers (TMMOB), the Social Forum of Istanbul and the Social Forum of Turkey (FST), created in June 2005, played an important role in the organization and coordination of these actions. Two political parties also took part in these social and political struggles: the ÖDP (the Freedom and Solidarity Party) and the DSIP (the Revolutionary Socialist Workers' Party), whose militants are also among the main movers of BAK and the FST. The former is an anti-capitalist left-wing party bringing together various tendencies and the latter is a Trotskyite party close to the Socialist Workers' Party in Britain.

The ecological struggles, particularly those against nuclear energy and genetically modified organisms (GMOs), also form part of this second grouping. On the nuclear question, the ecology movement managed to get a project to install a nuclear plant in Turkey suspended.

As for the anti–GMO platform, it organized a campaign in a number of towns in Anatolia to raise the awareness of farmers about the GMO threat and has collected some 100,000 signatures. It has also organized an information session in parliament and obtained a place in the parliamentary commission of enquiry on the subject, which is a new development for Turkey.

Identity struggles

The above two themes concern what we may call the Turkish alternative world movement. The third concerns identity struggles. The most emblematic are the Kurdish movement and the movement of Muslim women for freedom to wear the veil. The Kurdish demands are mostly expressed by the DTP (the People's Democratic Party), which was created recently by Leyla Zana and Orhan Dogan, former deputies who were in prison for ten years and liberated in 1995. But the DTP's ties with Abdullah Öcalan, leader of the Kurdistan Workers' Party (PKK) who is serving life imprisonment on an island near Istanbul, is currently preventing the DTP from acquiring legitimacy among the public. In fact, the riots that broke out in Diyarbakir in March/April 2006 can be explained by the control of Öcalan and the PKK over the Kurdish movements. The problem of democratization and the abandonment of violent and hierarchical structures has to be tackled by the Kurdish militants if their demands are to be seen as credible and reasonable in the eyes of the population.

The Muslim movements are in rather a different situation from that of the Kurds. In Turkey, Islamism, while being present in the political system, is under strict surveillance. It supports the contestation of the hegemony of a State secularism that is often seen as restrictive of individual freedoms, as illustrated by the prohibition of headscarves at the university. This is why some on the left and the moderate section of the Islamist movement come together in certain campaigns against a power that both parties consider to be oppressive.[1]

The centralizing inheritance

Social and political struggles in Turkey are very much influenced by the extreme centralism of the national political system. It should be underlined that the political culture, and even the experiences of the social movements and political forces, are not very enthused by 'a space that is open and horizontal, at the service of movements, trade-unions, NGOs and associations of all kinds, each engaged in its own way in its field of action and according to its methods' (Lelandais and Baykan 2004). This is why most of the struggles are carried out in the framework of political parties, trade unions and professional associations. Furthermore, the country's strictly national/political orientation makes it difficult for the radical left-wing organizations to make the links between the national and the global. The emergence of flexible coordination bodies with little hierarchy also has to take into account the inheritance of traditional norms that preach the cult of organization.

Efforts to organize local and national forums in Turkey contribute to the questioning of this state of affairs. The forum type of gathering is increasingly attracting the attention of civil society organizations, as it provides a platform for making themselves heard outside the State apparatus without the latter really feeling threatened. At the same time it renews the debate among the associations about their own form of organization, the European and other examples being under their scrutiny.

The alternative world movement is now a source of inspiration to trade-union struggles on behalf of social rights. For a long time the social struggle was confined to the national level and limited to strikes and negotiations with the government. Today, thanks to the alternative world movement, Turkish trade unions are beginning to make permanent links with unions in other countries and increasingly developing actions relevant to global themes.

But the alternative world movement in Turkey not only echoes the international character of the struggles or the connections between the issues in the different countries. It also poses questions about the relationships within Turkish society itself. It is no coincidence that the denunciation of United States hegemony through warfare is reflected locally in the denunciation of State hegemony. These two structures are implicitly allied. All these social struggles attribute responsibility to neoliberal globalization for a unique social domination, which is exercised over an ensemble of sectors of social life through concrete actors such as the IMF, the USA, the Turkish State, if not the army.

Limits and ambiguities of the democratic demands

While social and political struggles have grown considerably in recent years, they have not yet really found their place in Turkish society. Popular support remains limited. Since the anti-war movement, few struggles have really been supported by the majority of the population. This is due partly to the social and political structure of Turkey and partly to the internal problems of civil society. The demands for liberalization, democratization and respect for human rights provoke the State apparatus into a protective reflex in order to maintain its monopoly over politics and the economy. While economic liberalization does not meet many obstacles, benefiting particularly from the links between the political elites and the business world, as the Turkish employers' organization, TÜSIAD has pointed out, political liberalization progresses very slowly, mainly because it would express social demands against the neoliberal economy (Lelandais 2004).

There is also a paradox peculiar to Turkey. While the circles that are more open to modernization tend, through fear of Islamic fundamentalism, to range themselves on the side of the State, even if that means putting the brakes on democracy, the conservative circles line up regularly on the side of democracy in the hope of reducing the weight of the State on social life. The civil society organizations called 'progressive' are therefore close to the State, while the 'conservative' organizations are more inclined to be critical *vis-à-vis* the State.

Notes

1   In light of the transformation of the economy and of the State in the framework of neoliberal globalization, these peripheral forces must organize themselves or disappear. Originally created to give an autonomous aid, the new Islamic movements have become a source of resistance and an alternative to materialism. Thus the fields that were traditionally part of the public social services have often been taken over by private clubs and clinics organized by Muslim associations. In the present context Islam is not only an ensemble of religious rites, but also a social cement that links the 'communities' that have been abandoned by the neoliberal State (Pasha, 2001).

III Sub-Saharan Africa

Demba Moussa Dembélé

17
Struggles against
neoliberal policies in Africa

In Sub-Saharan Africa the struggles and campaigns against neoliberal policies intensified during 2005 and 2006.

Tony Blair, the British prime minister, wanted 2005 to be the 'Year of Africa' and presented himself as a champion of the 'war on poverty' on the continent.[1] However, in spite of roping in showbusiness personalities like Bono and Bob Geldof, this propaganda exercise ended in resounding failure. It could not have been otherwise, as the policies imposed by the World Bank, the International Monetary Fund and the World Trade Organization (WTO), which are supported by his government, have worsened the deterioration of living conditions for most Africans.[2] Hence the resistance being carried out by the social movements has intensified, especially in South Africa, Cameroon, Guinea-Conakry, Niger, Nigeria, Senegal and Zambia.

General and sectoral strikes, which have sometimes involved bloodshed, as in Guinea,[3] have been organized against unemployment and low wages, against the privatization of public services such as water and electricity, and against the threat of privatization of education and health. Peasant associations have also strongly opposed the trade liberalization policies that have severely affected agricultural prices. Associations like the Network of Organizations of Peasants and Producers of West Africa (ROPPA) have pressured governments to force them to protect peasant agriculture, particularly in cereal production and various fields (chickens, milk, tomatoes, etcetera) that are threatened by subsidized exports from the industrialized countries.

109

Land tenure and the urban environment are also important themes in the social struggles. In South Africa, Uganda, Senegal and Zimbabwe, social movements are organizing in slum areas and other unhealthy districts to claim the right to decent housing and a healthy environment. The question of human rights, particularly the fight against impunity, remains a major concern, as is illustrated by the Hissène Habré affair in Senegal.

The great continental and international campaigns[4]

There are also a number of continental and international campaigns. The campaign against the liberalization of services in the framework of the WTO was strengthened during the preparations for the Hong Kong conference in December 2005. Its aim was to force African countries into rejecting the pressures of the developed countries who were demanding that education and health be privatized.

As for the continent's debts, the G8's decision to annul the debts of fourteen African countries in the framework of the Highly Indebted Poor Countries (HIPC) Initiative has helped to galvanize the campaign for the unconditional cancellation of all the debts of the continent. This debt is odious and illegitimate and has already been repaid several times over. Moreover, the networks involved in this question are asking for an end to the policies of the IMF and the World Bank, whose conditionalities have devastated the African economies.[5]

The HIV/AIDS campaign has also revealed the responsibility of these institutions through their policies pushing for austerity and the privatization of public services, as well as the deterioration of health infrastructures and the working conditions of health personnel, above all in the countries that are most affected. The campaign against genetically modified organisms (GMOs) is growing, thanks partly to an increasing awareness of this question made possible by the struggles waged in several European countries and the pressures by the United States to force African countries to accept the consumption and cultivation of GMOs. In several countries, national coalitions have already been set up and in Western Africa, there is a very active anti-GMO network.

The tragedy of Ceuta and Melilla in September 2005 helped to strengthen solidarity among the social movements with the struggles being carried out by migrant workers in Europe. The tragedy and its resonance in France, Spain and Italy have enhanced the cooperation between the organizations of immigrant workers and the social movements within the African Social Forum (ASF). In fact, the immigration question has become one of the top concerns of the ASF. At Conakry (Guinea), in December 2005, and particularly at Bamako (Mali), during the Polycentric Social Forum, numerous plenaries and workshops were devoted to this subject, with the participation of representatives from immigrant workers' associations, who had come from Europe. Hostile demonstrations punctuated the visit of the French Interior Minister, Nicolas Sarkozy, to Mali and Benin during May 2006. And almost everywhere else, his law on 'selective immigration' has given rise to indignant reactions.[6] The solidarity campaigns on behalf of immigrants have been actively supported by European organizations (France, Italy, Spain) who work together with the immigrants' associations and the ASF to highlight the political dimension of this question, which is closely linked to the disastrous effects of neoliberal policies.

Extent of the struggles and campaigns and their challenges

All these struggles and campaigns figured prominently in the Polycentric Social Forum in Bamako. This forum showed the growing influence of the ideas and values defended by the African social movements, whose struggles have unquestionably contributed to the greater awareness of the dangers of neoliberal policies. As a result the movements have been able to strengthen their influence in debates about development in Africa and its relations with the countries of the North and international institutions. The impact of these struggles is already considerable in national, subregional, if not continental policies. A number of governments are beginning to question the validity of unbridled liberalization, all the more so as they can see how the countries of the North persist with their protectionist policies that prevent the access of African products to their markets.

There has been increased collective resistance by the African countries on trade issues within the WTO. On the debt question, official Africa completely adopted the discourse of the social movements with the appeal launched in 2005 by the African Union Commission, demanding cancellation of the debt of all African countries, without any conditions. A document drawn up by eminent personalities, including former finance ministers, who were brought together under the auspices of the Commission, stressed that 'many African countries have already reimbursed the owed amount several times ... the genesis and origins of certain debts are judged to be immoral, illegal/illegitimate and ambiguous'.[7]

A similar attitude seems to be developing about the Economic Partnership Agreements (EPAs), which the African trade ministers sharply criticized when they met in Nairobi (Kenya) in April 2006.[8]

All these positive signs are a testimony, not only to the growing influence of the ideas defended by the social movements, but above all to the disillusion concerning the neoliberal model, whose 'solutions' to Africa's development problems have led to a succession of failures that are causing the present deadlock.

One of the main challenges of the African movements is therefore to deepen the legitimacy crisis of this model and hence to reinforce the defiance of African countries towards it. Another challenge is to persuade these countries to explore people-based and democratic alternatives in the framework of a genuine African integration. To achieve these aims, the African social movements must strengthen their cohesion, their capacities for analysis and mobilizing people so as to be able to forge sustainable alliances with progressive political forces.

Notes

1   See 'Les masques africains de M. Anthony Blair', *Le Monde Diplomatique,* November 2005, p. 10.
2   See *African Development Indicators, 2005,* Washington: World Bank.
3   Some twenty people were killed by the police during the general strike declared by Guinea's main trade unions in mid-June 2006.
4   The campaign for the Millennium Development Goals is not included here, given its controversial character and the divisions it has created among the African social movements.
5   See Christian Aid, *The Economics of Failure: The Real Costs of 'Free' Trade for Poor Countries,* London, 2005.
6   See, for example, the remarks of the Senegalese writer Boubacar Boris Diop, 'Les nouveaux damnés de la terre', *Le Quotidien,* Dakar, 22 May 2006, pp. 6–7.

7   African Union, Meeting of Eminent Personalities, 2–3 May 2005, Dakar, Senegal, *Report,* p. 2.

8   The Nairobi Ministerial Declaration on Economic Partnership Agreements, Conference of African Trade Ministers, Nairobi, 12–14 April 2006.

Frank Khachina Matanga

18
Social movements and democratization in Kenya

The concept 'social movement' is arguably a very slippery one as it tends to incorporate a myriad of organizations. Even some of the so-called basic identifying characteristics of social movements such as group consciousness, group identity and solidarity (Heberle 1951) do not help much in setting social movements apart from other types of organizations. Thus the term has tended to connote different things to different people. For the purpose of this chapter, social movements are treated as part of civil society in that they are organizations formed outside the State focusing on specific political or social issues in society. These issues tend to be largely developmental in nature in that social movements tend to arise in close relation to the general problems of society's development.

Social movements and the State

The role of social movements in Kenya has become increasingly visible. In the early years of independence most of the social movements sprang up in response to the underdeveloped form of the State. It was in this spirit that the government of the day actively encouraged communities to participate in self-help efforts to achieve development goals (Republic of Kenya 1965). These self-help efforts from the grass-roots to the national level grew into what came to be known as the *harambee* movement. As a social movement, *harambee* literally meant the pulling together of resources for community development.

The era that followed the death in 1978 of Jomo Kenyatta (Kenya's first president) was mainly characterized by the entrenchment of increased authoritarianism under President Moi. The regime's deliberate efforts to limit the democratic space led to various unintended consequences, especially concerning the role of social movements. Among the fundamental changes introduced by the regime was the conversion of Kenya into a *de jure* one-party state. This was made possible by a hurried change in the national constitution in 1982 which in essence legally banned the formation and operation of opposition political parties that could challenge the ruling party at that time, the Kenya African National Union, KANU (Okumu and Holmquist, 1984; Adar 1998). Other undemocratic acts by the regime that served to reduce the political space included the passage of the act allowing detention without trial of perceived political opponents, and a severe clampdown on civil liberties such as freedom of the press, speech and assembly, among others.

In the absence of other organizations of a political nature (such as opposition parties) that could confront the excesses of the Moi State, a number of newly formed pressure groups took centre-stage. Among these organizations were the Forum for the Restoration of Democracy (FORD), the Moral Alliance for Peace (MAP), the Citizens' Coalition for Constitutional Change (4Cs), the National Council of Churches of Kenya (NCCK), and the National Convention Executive Council (NCEC). By combining their efforts and working together, these pressure groups spearheaded one of the most formidable social movements in post-colonial Kenya. In their efforts to democratize the State they recorded some stunning victories against the Moi regime. For instance, in 1991, the regime was compelled to re-introduce plural party politics through a constitutional amendment (Matanga 2000).

In the 2002 national elections, the combined opposition force (under the National Rainbow Coalition, NARC), with the support of progressive civil society, eventually captured State power and in the process brought to an end KANU's forty-year stranglehold on the country. NARC, under Kibaki, won the elections on a reform ticket. This fundamental victory carried with it the hopes of Kenyans for a better future in terms of a revived economy and democratized society. NARC promised, for instance, a new, more democratic national constitution and an end to the rampant corruption that had literally destroyed the economy. However, four years down the line since taking over power, the NARC government has proven itself to be a toothless dog and has failed to deliver on most of its election pledges. It is precisely because of this failure that Kenyan society has witnessed the current revival in the fortunes of social movements.

Desire for a new constitution on the part of a majority of Kenyans and the failure by the NARC government to deliver one is the current bone of contention. Whereas the majority seemed to favour the adoption of the Bomas draft constitution (a draft of the revised old constitution that was the end product of a series of workshops by parliamentarians and civil society representatives), some influential figures in the Kibaki government thought otherwise. Consequently, in January 2005, President Kibaki signed what has been described as a controversial bill, the Constitution of Kenya Review Bill. This allowed members of parliament to single-handedly alter the Bomas draft. Amidst opposition from civil society organizations and sections of parliamentarians, the Kibaki government went ahead and made fundamental amendments to the Bomas draft, resulting in what came to be known as the Wako draft constitution. The main issues of discord concerned the arrangements for sharing executive power, setting up a devolved government, and the *kadhis* (Muslim judges) and religious courts. In an attempt to resolve the impasse, the Kibaki government called for a national referendum, the first in Kenya's history, to gauge the popularity of the government-favoured Wako draft (*Standard*, 19 November 2005).

These were the circumstances that gave birth to one of Kenya's most prolific and radical social movements, the Orange Democratic Movement (ODM). Launched in Kisumu city on 25 September 2005, the ODM was an amalgamation of political parties and civil society organizations opposed to the Wako draft. The political parties in the ODM included KANU and the Liberal Democratic Party (LDP), while civil society organizations included the Yellow Movement, Katiba Watch, 4Cs and NCEC, among others (*Daily Nation*, 16 November and 23 November 2005). Among the main reasons put forward by the ODM for why the electorate should reject the Wako draft were the arguments that it was creating an imperial presidency by giving the presidency excessive powers, that it was going to establish two levels of government, district and national, with no coherent relationship between the two and no clear arrangement for the distribution of resources, and that it was vague on land issues (*Standard*, 19 November 2005). Key strategies employed by the ODM to mobilize the electorate to reject the proposed constitution included public rallies that attracted huge followings, and frequent announcements and advertisements in the print and electronic media.

The national referendum was eventually held on 21 November 2005. The outcome was a devastating and humiliating defeat for the Kibaki government. The government side could garner only 43 per cent of the total vote while the ODM scooped 53 per cent (*Daily Nation*, 23–30 November 2005). In clear black and white, the government-supported draft constitution had been rejected by the electorate, galvanized by the ODM. Although it began as a social movement there have been increasing moves to register the ODM as a political party to compete for political power come the 2007 national elections.

In summary, as already observed, in the early years of independence *harambee* constituted the main form of social movement in Kenya, and it was mainly geared towards achieving economic development goals. However, with time, social movements have become overtly politicized, with political goals aimed at confronting the State to open up the democratic space. In so doing, they have been largely successful, as in the case of the Orange Democratic Movement. The building blocks of social movements, political parties and civil society organizations, are of immense importance to the sustainability of democracy in Kenya.

Mahaman Tidjani Alou

19
Niger: Civil society activists reinject politics into public life

Over the past two decades, African countries have experienced a democratic effervescence without precedent in the history of the continent. While it was marked first of all by the struggle between parties to set up fairer and more open political orders, this effervescence – at least in the form it took in a country like Niger – reflected a search for deeper and more sustainable roots in democracy. This belief plays an important role in the social struggles that are upsetting the powers that be. In this respect Niger is a particularly interesting case as it introduces the question of social movements in the current African context of the depoliticization of major social issues.[1]

The turbulent political developments since 1991 and then the social demands put forward by civil society organizations in 2005 and 2006, in a stabilized institutional context, make this country an interesting example of the role played by the new social movements in relation to political power in Africa in the extremely volatile context of globalization. The aim here is not to make a comprehensive study of the situation and still less to explain it. Basically it is to make a succinct description of a particular case that shows one aspect of the political changes that are happening today on the African continent.

During the 1990s Niger experienced great political and institutional instability. In the twelve years after the death of General Seyni Kountché in 1987, there were four republics, two military *coups d'état* (the last, in 1999, ended with the assassination of a president of the republic), several military mutinies, continual strikes by workers – and all this while Niger's economic performance was weak.[2] The fifth republic, which was established at the end of 1999, has proved to be a model of stability in the recent political history of the country. Its institutions have worked. The electoral mandates (presidential and legislative) that it set up have completed their terms and the new institutions have settled down to a regular routine.

At least that is what could have been imagined after the last presidential and legislative elections at the end of 2004. These gave a clear majority to the government, to the benefit of the outgoing president. But then there was an outburst of protest, organized by certain organizations from 'civil society'. This movement, through its abilities to negotiate, obliged the government to create new relationships with its social partners. Thus there was a new pattern in politics, in which the presence and activism of civil society had a strong influence, for its representatives were far from being mere figureheads or exhibitionists. They came to be fully accepted as participants in the political arena.

A great protest movement has emerged

Following the adoption of a law amending the law on finance of October 2004, new fiscal measures were taken by the government.[3] These integrated several commonly consumed products (rice, milk, sugar, flour, wheat, cooking oil, etcetera), seen as 'basic necessities', into the category of products that are subject to value added tax (VAT), which is 19 per cent. These measures were also extended to the consumption allocations of water and electricity reserved for low-income households (up to 15 cubic metres for water and up to 50 kilowatts an hour for electricity). They were vigorously denounced by associations promoting human rights and by the trade union on the grounds they would raise inflation and increase poverty among those already underprivileged.

Officially, these reforms aimed at producing more finance for the State and allowing Niger to conform to convergence criteria of the West African Economic and Monetary Union (UEMOA). But among the reactions there was a clear sense of injustice, that 'it is always the poor who pay'. A social front was thus created to rally all the civil society organizations to force the government to abrogate its fiscal measures.   The coalition also invited the government to reduce its standard of living which was felt to be too extravagant. It was in this context that a number of associations decided to create the Equity/Quality of Life Coalition against the Cost of Living, at the beginning of 2005.

The first protest movements were conducted under the auspices of the leaders of the consumer association of Niger (Orconi), the association SOS Kandadji and the Committee for Reflection and an Independent Orientation for the Safeguarding of Democratic Gains (Croisade). To this group was added the Democratic Coordination of Niger's Civil Society (CDSCN) which federates several different associations. The setting up of the Equity/Quality of Life Coalition against the Cost of Living marked the point of departure for a series of protests directly opposing the governmental measures contained in the amended law on finance. The actions of this vast movement were to induce the government, after lengthy negotiations, to go back on its decisions.

Such success roots this new structure in the political arena, bringing different visions to the management of public affairs. The Coalition intend to take further action. They will concentrate on the demands for reductions in the price of electricity, water and oil products. Once again, the government will be forced to take into account these social demands, that are widely shared, by creating a forum to negotiate with the new organization that leads the new forms of protest against the high cost of living.

New mobilization techniques

The Equity/Quality of Life Coalition against the Cost of Living has shown its considerable capacity to mobilize people, particularly on two occasions (though not without certain difficulties), and in setting up a framework for dialogue with the government for finding solutions to the problems being raised. The stages of struggle were gradual. First there were meetings and marches, which attracted large crowds. These high-visibility demonstrations were then publicized through the press which itself took part in the movement. And then, to crown their activities, they launched 'dead town' and even 'dead country' operations. A 'dead town' is one without taxis, without street vendors, without open trading centres, without markets, without cars. For a whole day, the population remains at home. There are no services because workers are either participating in the movement or blocked at home for lack of transport to go to work. It is thus a means of struggle that involves a whole town. The 'dead country' operation more or less successfully involved the whole country, which was affected, at least episodically, in a situation of generalized standstill.

This strategy used by the Coalition proved effective. Its main achievement has been to make the new association a valid interlocutor, conveying social demands and capable of negotiating over them with the government, in the framework of negotiations specially created to treat the questions raised by the protest movements.

Profiles of the new militant associations

The actors who are emerging are not militants from the political parties or from the trade unions, from whom they seek to distinguish themselves. They call themselves association militants who, while carrying out various projects, commit themselves through the creation of a coalition of associations to struggle against the cost of living. It is a huge programme which *a priori* may concern all sectors of government policy. Often these militants issue from the student movement in which they were activists during their youth, and they subsequently participated in the struggles that led to the victory for democracy in Niger.

The African regimes that have emerged from the democratic processes have not integrated such actors into official positions, or very rarely. Many of them remain militants, well organized in their structures and often well connected to international association networks. They have often had experience in running press businesses and in human rights advocacy. They face the new regimes that are purportedly democratic as the guardians of values that they have helped to acquire and implant in a country like Niger after a long period of authoritarian rule.

Through their struggles they have downgraded the political parties which, however, they try to stimulate through new alliances. Through their actions they re-inject politics into public life, at the same time as the conditionalities of the international financial institutions have both gradually ejected it, and disqualified parliaments, which then resemble mere ratification bodies for the policies decided by government. The leaders of the Coalition are careful not to proclaim political ambitions, but the very logic of their actions, by attacking public policy and the

neoliberal options that underlie them – does it not lead them inevitably
to take up positions on governmental orientations? Time will reveal the
destiny of these new actors and the forces and weaknesses of the
dynamics that they are trying to set in motion, as well as the transforma-
tions in modes of governance brought about by their actions.

Notes

1 The growing influence of the international financial institutions in deciding
   policy in the economic and social sectors has removed major social issues from
   decision-making by national political actors. See M. Alou Tidjani (2001) 'La
   globalisation: l'Etat africain en question', *Afrique contemporaine*, July-Septem-
   ber, No. 199, pp 11–24.
2 For many years the UNDP reports and its Human Development Index
   regularly classed Niger among the poorest countries on the planet.
3 This law had several fiscal sections. We are concerned here only with those
   that have received most media attention.

Ian Taylor

20
Botswana's civil society:
weak and under threat

Botswana's growth record has been impressive and, because it has practised formal democracy since independence, the country has been repeatedly dubbed the 'African Miracle'. However, the fairness of the democratic system in a country is affirmed not only by what happens at the polling stations on the day of elections but by the broader milieu within which the political process plays itself out. It should be noted that since independence the country has only ever been ruled by one political party: the Botswana Democratic Party (BDP). The strength of civil society in any country is always a fair indicator of the real nature of democracy in a country, yet, when one looks at Botswana, its civil society is revealed to be weak and under threat from the government.

Part of civil society's effectiveness is access to information, freedom to campaign, and equal and fair access to the media. However, with the exception of small localized private radio stations – such as Gabz FM – the electronic media is government-controlled. The national radio station Radio Botswana is a government mouthpiece, and so is the only daily newspaper, the *Daily News*. Although opposition activities are covered, the overall perception of the contents of such media products is that the government is given much greater weight. There are, however, a number of private weekly periodicals which maintain considerable independence from the ruling party. It is these journals that have in the past exposed government corruption scandals.

Unfortunately, the immaturity of the Botswana press and its propensity for scandal and trivia centred around personalities undermine much of the potential that the media might have. The independent press frequently publishes gossip and innuendo as fact, rarely bothering to check stories, and sharp political analysis is rare. Having said that, the government has done little to promote or strengthen media freedom, diversity and expansion. It instead continues to thrive on restrictive media legislation, bureaucratic red tape and unclear policies.

A number of restrictive laws continue to impinge on the free operation of the media in the country. Examples are: the National Security Act of 1986, which gives the State potentially repressive power to penalize legitimate reporting; the Anthropological Act of 1967, which restricts research and limits access to information; and Section 59 of the Penal Code, which provides for penalties for causing 'public alarm'. In addition, the Economic Crimes and Corruption Act of 1994 restricts both access to and coverage of information regarding ongoing police investigations into corruption allegations.

It is quite evident that within the ruling BDP there is disdain for opposing views and lack of tolerance for such opinions to be aired. In 2002 the Minister of Presidential Affairs and Public Administration, Daniel Kwelagobe, castigated Botswana Television (BTV, already government-owned and widely perceived as being under government editorial control) for broadcasting 'insults' spoken by an opposition leader against the government. Kwelagobe asserted that BTV should have cut the 'offensive' parts of the news item and he demanded that BTV sanitize what they broadcast to the public. Such outbursts came on top of an earlier spat with BTV which saw the editor of news and current affairs, Christopher Bishop, resign after the Director of Information and Broadcasting, Andrew Sesinyi, forbade Bishop from broadcasting a documentary on Mariette Bosch, a South African who had been convicted by a Botswana court of murder, and executed. The instruction for this allegedly came straight from Vice-President Ian Khama.

Government intentions regarding the media in Botswana were expressed in the draft Mass Media Communications Bill. This would have profound implications for media freedom and democracy in Botswana. Among its strictures is a requirement for the registration of publications as well as for the accreditation of local and foreign journalists. The recommendation that a media council should be established, to be chaired by government-appointed persons, and the stated aim of introducing fines for every offence and prosecution (and up to three years in jail for convicted journalists) was also included within the proposed Bill, as was the proposed right of senior police officers to seize any publication. Currently, the draft is with the government and has not yet been introduced. Its intention, though, seems crystal clear. The seriousness of this for the credibility of Botswana's democracy is profound.

Threats to media independence and media surveillance of the government and elites are profoundly amplified in the context of a polity such as Botswana, where civil society is very weak. Comparatively speaking, civil society groups in Botswana are not as fully developed as in other African countries. This reality may be partly attributable to the political and economic stability that has prevailed since independence. Furthermore, the lack of any meaningful 'struggle' for independence and the concomitant absence of a tradition of questioning – combined with an essentially top-down traditional culture of acquiescence before one's superiors – may explain the relative weakness and disorganized nature of civil society.

Just as the BDP is adept at co-option, the government in Botswana has also been active in initiating the formation of organizations within 'civil society'. As a result, through this corporate strategy, the State has appropriately defined the role and functions of each organization and circumscribed these so that it becomes easy to label some respectable and isolate others as 'political'. The government exhibits highly undemocratic tendencies to portray those organs of civil society it deems beyond its control as foreign stooges, and has not been shy to play the race card against any foreign supporters of civil society in an adversarial relationship with Gaborone. Citizens who stand up to the government are quickly regarded as traitors and foreign agents.

During the campaign to protect the Bushmen from being removed from the Kalahari, Gaborone's Foreign Minister, Mompati Merafhe, was quoted as describing Survival International as 'our enemy, and an enemy of Botswana', whilst the Director of the Remote Area Dweller Programme (in charge of providing services to the Bushmen) declared that by enlisting the help of international NGOs the Bushmen were 'highly seditious' and that 'someone is going to have to answer'. When it was discovered that some Bushmen had been given satellite phones to enable them to be in contact with NGOs this was seen as categorical proof that the Bushmen were indeed akin to an indigenous fifth column.

Suspicion of foreign involvement, particularly if it involves 'sensitive' topics such as the Bushmen situation, readily provokes a clampdown. For example, the Kuru Development Trust, which is a well-known NGO working with the Bushmen, had their co-ordinator, Bram le Roux, declared a prohibited immigrant in 1993. And in 2005 Professor Kenneth Good was deported from Botswana for writing (with this author) a paper that criticized presidential powers. Good, who had taught at the University of Botswana for fifteen years, was the most vociferous academic operating within civil society. Yet he was expelled with no warning. And the personal experience of this author indicates that the government has absolutely no interest in engaging with any actors from civil society unless they are yes men who will say what the government wants to hear.

In conclusion, civil society in Botswana is weak and is readily co-opted into State structures. It lacks a strong grassroots base and is only prepared to work within the parameters considered permissible by the State – and not beyond. It is dominated by relatives of the elite class and often seems to be a mere hobby, rather than a vocation. Consensus politics and the construction of BDP hegemony post-1966 have created a relatively stable political milieu. This has meant that it is fairly easy for the government to delegitimize any political expression outside the hegemonic agenda set by the BDP.

Despite Botswana's reputation as a bastion of democracy and tolerance, its civil society is probably the weakest in the whole of southern Africa. This is the result of a government that has been successful in portraying a myth to the outside world, which foreign observers (particularly academics) have been all too happy to accept – so desperate for a 'success story' in Africa that they turn a blind eye to what really occurs in the 'African Miracle'.

Sylvestre Kambaza

21
Political transition and civil society
in the Democratic Republic of the Congo

In August 1988, following dissension between the national and the foreign 'liberators' who had toppled the Mobutu regime the previous year, a second 'liberation' war broke out. This war, which lasted more than five years, divided the country into three zones of influence (East, West and North), led by warlords, with the circulation of goods and people being restricted between them. The actors of civil society, from all provinces, refused to accept this *de facto* balkanization set up by the belligerents. At risk of their lives, non-military and non-governmental organizations continued to exchange visits, meeting sometimes in Kinshasa, sometimes outside the country, to discuss and organize what to do to put an end to the war.

The war did in fact end in June 2003 but it, together with the long dictatorship that preceded it, destroyed almost all the social and economic infrastructures that had been inherited from the colonial epoch. Thus we are in a country that has boundless potentialities that have not been exploited, and that has been barbarously pillaged by the former belligerents, now in power in complicity with their allies in some neighbouring countries or certain Western companies. The overwhelming majority of the population is destitute, having been abandoned to their fate. They have had to develop various ways of survival without the help of the state or charities. There has been a mushrooming of civil associations, acting in most sectors of social life, to fill the gap left by the politicians and the public administration.

These associations come from different parts of Congolese civil society: the churches, development NGOs, human rights NGOs, women's organizations, youth movements, trade unions, businesmen's organizations, cultural associations. They have found ways of exchanging information throughout the country, both vertically and horizontally, from the grassroots to the national level. They have developed means of communication, unofficial and clandestine, beyond the reach of the belligerents in order to avoid censorship of their messages of struggle and social resistance.

While they carried on with their social and economic activities to relieve the population, the associations also invested in the search for peace. Thus they have become an indispensable part of Congolese society and recognized as such, both by different belligerents and the institutions of the African Union and the United Nations involved in bringing peace to the country. They were invited to all the inter-Congolese negotiations which led to the signing of peace agreements in December 2002. Nevertheless, these negotiations also created an upheaval in civil society. Rather than continuing to play the role of counterpower and arbiter between the different political actors, most of the delegates, after the negotiations had ended, accepted political positions during the transition phase that followed. These included political mandates within the government and in institutions that were supporting the transition, as well as in parliament. This participation of civil society in sharing power put it in a situation of being both judge and judged.

Civil society is now divided into two large groups: on the one hand the actors who have come to power and, on the other, those who remained to work in their own organizations. This has greatly weakened Congolese civil society. Some of its most well-known figures now have to defend the political institutions in which they work. They have to face those who have kept their freedom of action and who create pressure for these institutions to respect their commitments to the population. As a result of this bipolarization of civil society, it gradually became discredited in public opinion and also in the eyes of other political actors, who no longer believed in its capacity to mobilize people. This did not however prevent a number of associations from continuing the fight for the political transition to be terminated by the given deadline and for the organization of free and transparent legislative elections. National voting – the first round of the presidential and legislative elections – duly took place on 30 July 2006.

As was feared, the civic education of the population was not a real priority either for the government or for the independent election commission (CEI) – and even less so for the political parties. To try to fill the vacuum, civil society organizations were very active in different ways, in preparing citizens for the elections, in monitoring the vote, as well as in accepting the results. They set up a 'joint framework for monitoring the elections' which included the large associations and non-governmental and non-partisan platforms, with their branches in different parts of the country.

More than 10,000 observers, trained by socially committed civil society, were thus sent out round the country, even into the less accessible areas. Their reports relayed the local realities: the elections were held to be credible and transparent, in spite of certain organizational weaknesses and other irregularities observed. This helped considerably to get the results accepted by the population and among the candidates throughout the country, except in Kinshasa where the political and media manipulation was very strong, creating murderous confrontations between the camps of the two candidates for the presidency, Joseph Kabila and Jean-Pierre Bemba, who competed in the second round in November, with the former gaining the majority of votes.

In conclusion, in spite of internal weaknesses, mainly due to the thirst for power and money of certain members, civil society has greatly contributed in recent years to maintaining the unity of the country, which extends over two million square kilometres and has been continually subjected to and devastated by predatory wars. Civil society has managed to develop various methods of resistance which obliged different political actors to negotiate peace and agree on a timetable for democratization through the organization of free elections at the end of a turbulent three-year political transition phase.

Despite this non-negligible achievement, civil society has, however, emerged weakened from this struggle by having agreed to exercise political functions during the political transition, instead of playing, on behalf of the population, its watchdog role over the (in)action of the political leaders. Nevertheless, in spite of this backsliding among the higher echelons, most of the social organizations that had genuine roots in society continue their work of civic education among the population and of exercising pressure on the authorities to ensure that, after the elections, they respect their commitments to the economic and political reconstruction of the country, grounded on sovereign and democratic principles.

Femi Aborisade

22
Nigeria: The ambiguities of the social movement

The character of the social movements in Nigeria in the period under review was determined by the increasing failure of the State to guarantee the basic means of decent living for the people. Poverty levels have been lowered by the continual imposition of neoliberal policies, which absolve the State of any role in the economy.

The socio-political conditions generated by the failure of the State provided fertile ground for the activities of social movements. The most recurrent indices of the failed State could be listed as follows: massive job losses; labour casualization; increases in the prices of petroleum products; poverty wages; sale of public housing units and eviction of thousands of civil servant occupants; non-payment of gratuities and pensions; non-involvement of unions in discussions over severance packages in privatized companies; the commercialization of education; denial of the right to unionize; dispossession of peasants of their lands, etcetera. There has also been resistance by communal, ethnic and religious formations that feel alienated and threatened by the hostile State. However, the most dominant issue, which has taken centre-stage in the relations between the State and civil society in recent times, is the situation in the Niger Delta, where individuals, groups and whole communities continue to react, often violently, in response to the violent process of oil exploration.

The aborted attempt by President Obasanjo to induce the National Assembly to amend the Constitution to facilitate the extension of his tenure for a third term also contributed to a sharp rise in ethnic nationalism across the country and raised issues of individual and group rights, which threatened the survival of Nigeria's civil rule. The political process was therefore characterized by brutal violation of basic rights of expression, association, assembly and action. The common refrain was that no rally or public meeting against government actions and policies could be held 'without police permit', while the elected state governors of Bayelsa and Oyo were forcefully and unconstitutionally removed from office. The police and stone-throwing and machete-wielding political thugs attacked rallies organized by pro-democracy groups. Security agents raided media and publishing houses, seizing tapes of recorded programmes and copies of publications that were critical of the tenure extension agenda.

All the above violations form part of the trend towards a steady descent into a neo-fascist state. The Bank and Other Financial Institutions (Amendment) Bill, sent to the National Assembly in April 2006, symbolizes the entrenchment of authoritarianism, rather than democratic norms, in Nigeria. The Bill seeks to criminalize trade unionism in the banking sector. If it is passed into law without challenge, it would be applied to other industries. The new Trade-Unions (Amendment) Act 2005 permits, for the first time since 1978, the registration of multiple central labour organizations, but it criminalizes the picketing of companies, which is unprecedented.

In these circumstances, how could the roles of the social movements be assessed with a view to strengthening the civil society in its striving to build a new world, where respect for fundamental rights is the essence of governance?

Although the socio-political conditions have produced many social movements, reflecting from the issues identified above, the process has not created strong mass-based coalitions. Struggles are often waged in sectional and fractionalized ways, so that their impact is limited. What are the reasons for this? First, the leadership of the social movements is not sufficiently political, in terms of sharing the perspective of political solutions to problems. The predominant perspective is that of pressure groups which rely on influencing political power-wielders to introduce changes, their goal seeming to be limited to winning some marginal concessions and not obtaining political power. That is why the opposition pro-democracy groups in PRONACO (Pro-National Conference), which organized the People's Conference in 2006, in contrast to that organized by the federal government in 2005, posited that any self-appointed people-oriented government in the future could implement the model constitution and resolutions they had passed.

In fact, some leaders of the social movements dread the mass movement just as the ruling classes do. For this reason, there is a tendency on their part to demobilize, rather than mobilize massively for popular struggles. Where they are compelled to embark on mass strike actions, they are eager to reach compromise and call off actions. Rather than using street protest, they more often than not settle for 'sit-at-home' action, thus depriving the struggle of the active inputs of its members. So the rank and file cannot feel that there is any possibility of influencing the course of history and bringing about fundamental change. The concern to assure the ruling class that there is no intention to upset the status quo results in a tendency not to raise non-economic, political demands about the termination of the tenure of political regimes. All these factors influenced the September 2005 strikes against the anti-fuel price rise organized by the coalition of the three central labour organizations, along with human rights and pro-democracy organizations – called the Labour and Civil Society Organization (LASCO). The leadership of the social movements therefore often acts as a brake on the movement.

Another important factor militating against the growth and self-activity of Nigerian social movements is that the leading non-governmental organizations that have played key roles in the democratization process rely mainly on foreign funding by international agencies that are themselves funded by imperialist governments. They are usually forbidden from raising certain political issues.

The depoliticization of social movements in Nigeria also has to do with the desperate material poverty of the rank-and-file social activists. They are often driven into action out of necessity, in order to survive. They embark on struggles not out of commitment to any principles or ideals of changing society, but simply because they cannot otherwise survive. The advantage is that this stimulates zeal, courage and determination to unite, fight and win; the disadvantages include having limited perspectives and the seeking of immediate palliatives to solve the problem of economic survival, devoid of concern for any long-term political solutions. This explains the phenomenon of hostage-taking for ransom that is rampant in the oil-producing Niger Delta, as well as 'arms for cash' deals, acceptance of licences to drill oil by companies fronting for some militant groups, etcetera.

Moreover, there are reactionary twists to the development of the social movements that tend to weaken its cohesion and unity. The killings and kidnappings of oil workers in the Niger Delta and the intra- and inter-poor conflicts, particularly among some ethnic and communal organizations, undermine the effectiveness of the broad social movement. Of all regional inter- and intra-poor conflicts in the country, those in the Niger Delta appear most intractable. In reality, some of the community-based militant groups are inspired and nurtured by highly placed business and political cliques who engage in oil bunkering. The groups are thus nothing but pawns in the inter- and intra-party/elite conflicts.

These reactionary twists in the social movements do not mean that there are no independent organizations carrying out self-motivated activities to resist social exclusion and genocidal repression by the State. But, for the social movement in Nigeria to move forward, the need is to create powerful mass-based coalitions, not just among the leadership of organizations but also among local branches. There is also a need to draw up charters of demands articulating the concerns of all interest groups among the dispossessed. Their underlying principle should be opposition to neoliberal policies and defence of universally recognized fundamental rights. This would remove the present anomaly in the protests of the social movements who, rather than fighting the causes of the problems, often attack only the symptoms. For example, they struggle against increases in the price of petroleum products and do not oppose the principle of deregulation and liberalization of the oil sector. In the same way, trade unions fight against casualization, retrenchment and for the collective determination of severance packages in privatized enterprises, rather than also opposing privatization in principle.

Yves Alexandre Chouala

23
Cameroon:
Is its civil society 'tainted'?

The directory of non-governmental organizations in Cameroon, compiled with the aid of the United Nations Development Programme in 1997, listed 206 organizations that were officially registered in the country. According to a survey carried out by the National Governance Programme of Cameroon during 2004, there are some 55,502 registered associations, composed of groups for common initiatives, savings and credit cooperatives, community associations and advocacy groups. The survey found that 78 per cent of the active population was involved in the association movement. These two studies, carried out within an interval of seven years, show that there has been an exponential evolution and a 'densification' of Cameroonian civil society. It contributes to the creation of a civil space and – better still – a civil society that is distinguishable from the public sector of official governance and the political scene.

The main characteristic of civil society in Cameroon is that it is clearly oriented towards being a social movement promoting self-reliance, providing social services that the State is increasingly incapable of supplying. It is thus involved in the social struggle for daily survival as well as in the transformation of political, economic and social structures in favour of the underprivileged. The main social fields in which the NGOs are engaged illustrate this tendency: the war on poverty, sustainable development, health and environment training and upgrading capacities, human rights and governance, peace and security, etcetera.

This orientation of helping people to help themselves is considerably diminishing the political consciousness and capacity of Cameroonian civil society, which is in complete antithesis to taking a critical approach and questioning of the leaders. This is not to say that civil society does not make political demands, but to stress that its mobilization capacity and political influence are weak. Its blossoming has not brought about any real restructuring of public opinion, nor has it constituted a public space for sufficiently critical discussion in order to shake the hegemonic domination of the leadership. The tendency is even for there to be a collusion between civil society and political interests.

Fragmenting and instrumentalizing civil society

Thus it is that in Cameroon there is not one but several civil societies: the civil society of power, the civil society of opposition, and the civil society of the non-affiliated. In other words each socio-political camp has its own civil society. Many of the associations and organizations are just excrescences of the political parties: they relay their party's discourses, promote its interests and defend its views and positions. Hence the epithet 'tainted civil society' was coined by a Cameroonian analyst.

This fragmentation of civil society on socio-political lines is responsible for its feeble capacity to constitute a community to plead the cause of social change and mobilize the citizenship. The civil society does not have a sufficiently strong voice to bring about political and institutional change. Nor does it put forward proposals for alternatives or federating and mobilizing utopias.

Another factor that influences the social and political effectiveness of Cameroonian civil society is that it is instrumentalized politically and economically by actors seeking power and resources. Many NGOs and associations serve mainly to help the political rise of their promoters. There are ministers in the government on behalf of civil society. These organizations are increasingly being used just to obtain additional financial resources and create private fortunes in the economic reconversion of the old politico-bureaucratic dignitaries.

The NGOs are thus turning themselves into agencies for obtaining finance. Their position as financial intermediaries leads to aggressive fighting between them for project funding. There also exist NGO professionals who live off 'non-profit' activities – and very comfortably too. Here, as elsewhere in Africa, the proliferation of non-governmental organizations is less a sign of the vitality of an emerging civil society than a simple, pragmatic move in the strategy for obtaining funding. The training of 'apolitical associations' that are 'non-profit' is one of the many means used to achieve upward social mobility, to recompose the elites and to amass private fortunes.

Lack of roots and legitimacy

It is evident that these compromises have had negative effects on the capacity of civil society to wage social resistance. In the first place, the logic of funding means that organizations search for projects that are operationally legitimate, requiring technical expertise. Moreover, they are not socially representative, which is the only guarantee of their popular legitimacy. The bodies that form part of Cameroonian civil society seem to be mostly empty structures, without any real capacity to mobilize people. The only ones that do are those depending on family or community ties as a framework for action. And in these associations that are bound by family or ties of affection, the orientation is more for reinforcing family traditions and the survival of community solidarity than for dismantling oppressive politico-economic structures.

The lack of representativity and legitimacy of civil society bodies also leads them into mounting activities (or 'struggles') that are superficial and inappropriate for the grassroots. Quite often in Cameroon, non-governmental networks mobilize to defend a 'local' cause without the local people being involved at all. In other words, the NGOs make themselves into spokespeople for local populations without having any mandate from them. Hence their 'struggles' are ineffective: they are simply mantras or slogans without having any mobilizing effects on the grassroots.

Secondly, the professional, operational and technician-oriented approach of Cameroonian civil society bodies limits their militant potential. This is why advocacy and lobbying constitute most of their work and they cannot be considered as structures for defending the excluded against the injustice of political and economic decisions. Nor do they appear to be a means of channeling public opinion that would aim at exercising political pressure on matters that affect the daily life of the population.

The seminar/workshops of 'education for development', or 'reinforcing capacity building' or 'conscientization' seem more like budgetary expedients than genuine advocacy actions. In fact, advocacy should be at the very centre of the expression of resistance against the injustice of the politico-economic project of globalization because it helps to alert world public opinion about these injustices and demands that they be corrected. Cameroonian civil society does not show great capacity to resist inequalities of any kind. Rather resistance here is passive and takes the form, like a simple visiting card, of the discourse of the large international organizations.

Thus the Cameroonian organizations are very tenuously attached to the world social movement that is now embodied by the alternative world movement. There is no national social forum worthy of the name. If the present tendencies of Cameroonian civil society persist, unlike those in Brazil or Bolivia it will not generate spaces for popular resistance that is capable of upsetting the position of those who are currently dominant. In order to overcome these tendencies, Cameroonian organizations will have to rise to three major challenges: transparency, representativeness and democratization.

Fiona White

24
Social movements in South Africa:
The Soweto Electricity Crisis Committee

Social movements in South Africa have continued to grow and diversify since their emergence after the end of apartheid in 1994. Their activities were primarily in response to a need to confront poverty and inequality in many disadvantaged areas of the country. Inequality in South Africa is extreme. A mere 6 per cent of South Africa's population accounts for over 40 per cent of its income, and nearly 50 per cent of the population currently falls below the national poverty line.[1] The move to formal democracy which came with the end of apartheid did not bring with it socio-economic equality for a large part of the population. This has resulted in many communities feeling marginalized and disempowered, especially with regard to service delivery. Alongside challenging government's service delivery, social movements also oppose the neoliberal capitalist path they believe is encapsulated in the government's economic strategy. Many social movements therefore are against privatization, corporate power and an uncontrolled market.

Since 2005 the established social movements in the country, such as the Treatment Action Campaign (fighting for HIV/AIDS treatment) and the Anti-Privatization Forum (an umbrella organization assisting community movements in Gauteng province), have continued to campaign and consolidate their support base. New movements have also arisen, especially in the area of housing, which have added to growing pressure on the State to provide adequate and sustainable shelter for the poor. One example is Abahlali Base Mjondolo, a shack dwellers' movement based in Durban. Their campaign to improve the living conditions of poor people in Durban has received steadily increasing support,[2] while a movement that has continued to consolidate its support base and find new ways of campaigning for change is the Soweto Electricity Crisis Committee (SECC). It is an instructive example of why social movements have arisen in South Africa, how they operate, and what their impact is.

The SECC was formed in mid-2000 after national electricity provider Eskom's move to privatization and a consequent rise in electricity prices of 47 per cent in 1999. Township residents began forming small spontaneous groups to fight on this issue. By 2001, when 20,000 houses a month were being disconnected from the electricity supply, the nascent organization called a mass meeting in Soweto which coalesced these smaller groups into a formal movement.

As the organization originated to challenge government delivery of electricity in Soweto, one of its first programmes was Operation Khanyisa (light) which reconnected electricity supply in Soweto. Local residents were trained to do this and within six months over 3,000 people were reconnected to the grid. SECC's first leader, Trevor Ngwane, believes that they 'turned what was a criminal deed from the point of view of Eskom into an act of defiance. It was good tactics and good politics'.[3] The organization has subsequently broadened its concerns and called for greater changes, including equal access in many areas of basic service provision including water, housing, education and transport, as well as rejecting the privatization of State services. For Ngwane, 'There needs to be a change in the system so there is more say for ordinary people ... over these issues. We support the principle of people before profit'.[4] To this end the organization formally adopted a vision of socialism, although there is ongoing debate as to the type of socialism they want.

The SECC initially operated in five areas in Soweto. However they now claim to have thirty-two branches across the township and estimate they have some 7,000 members, although it is difficult to measure this precisely.[5] Certainly support does fluctuate, specifically with regard to marches. But weekly meetings, involving branch representatives, consistently attract several hundred participants. Their agendas are long and include discussions on globalization and Third World debt as well as individual members presenting their household

electricity or water concerns. The leadership claims to be closely connected to and fairly representing its grassroots constituency. Indeed it is
easy for any member to approach the leadership, which has an accessible
office, and there is the opportunity to speak at the weekly meetings.
The organization employs a diverse range of strategies but its 'main
strategy is direct action'.[6] Often in conjunction with the Anti-
Privatization Forum, it organizes protest marches, as Ngwane believes it
is important to use strategies that draw on the power and experience of
the working class. Moreover it is felt that as diverse a range of people as
possible should be involved in fighting their campaigns. For this reason
they do not focus on tactics such as negotiations which require only a
small, specialized team.

Along with mass action the SECC also promotes the boycotting of
payments for services and, once relationships with unions are stronger,
hopes to organize stay-aways, similar to anti-apartheid general strikes.
The organization also engages with democratic institutions such as the
Human Rights Commission and the Constitutional Court. They are
wary of using the legal system as 'courts are State courts' but on occasion
have found themselves with no alternative. According to Ngwane, 'we
will use anything in the democratic context to further our cause'.[7]

In 2006 it was decided to adopt a new strategy: contesting local government elections. They wish to use elections to 'expose bourgeois
democracy' and 'the capitalist class agenda of the African National
Congress (ANC) government'.[8] Standing under the banner of Operation Khanyisa, the SECC won a proportional representation seat on
Johannesburg City Council. They recognize that their impact within
the council will be limited. However, by forming alliances with other
small parties they plan to table motions supporting the aims of their
social movement. They also hope that having a city councillor will
increase knowledge about the movement in the region and that their
support base will grow.[9]

Several 'small victories' have been claimed by SECC since its
inception. The SECC feels Operation Khanyisa in 2001 was a success
not only because it reconnected Sowetans to the electricity grid, but
also because it attracted the attention of city officials, councillors and
Eskom. Eskom did eventually reconsider its position, announcing a
moratorium on cut-offs, and in December 2002 the Public Enterprise
Minister offered a partial amnesty on arrears. SECC's campaigning

against pre-paid water meters has also had some impact on service delivery, with Johannesburg Water acknowledging, 'They keep us on our toes'.[10] The organization still has a long road to travel, however, before its medium-term demands for flat-rate monthly pricing and no privatization are met – not to mention their long-term call for socialism.

The organization also faces an ongoing challenge: they have a very antagonistic relationship with the government, and members have on many occasions been arrested and jailed. However, the leadership reacts positively to the ANC's hostility, believing that when the ANC accuses them of being anti-ANC, it is in fact promoting the SECC cause. Regardless of past setbacks, it sees itself as gaining strength as an opposition force to the ANC. Ngwane believes that it is 'becoming more like a civic; people come to us with their problems because we are the official opposition in Soweto now'.[11]

It is doubtful that the SECC is really the 'official opposition' in Soweto. However its strength does not diminish and its strategies are becoming more sophisticated. As a social movement it is well organized and on many occasions it has successfully mobilized a constituency in the township to fight its cause. It has also successfully highlighted the electricity crisis facing many Sowetans and forced the government at least to acknowledge service provision difficulties in the township. In choosing strategy it tends to use old-style, anti-apartheid politics, although with a post-apartheid cause and in a democratic context. Thus the SECC employs the democratic spaces available to it, such as the local council, the legal system and the media. The coming years will show whether it remains a relatively coherent, sustainable movement, expanding its support base, or becomes fragmented, losing the critical voice it currently provides.

Many social movements in South Africa have followed a path similar to that of the SECC. They have coalesced to fight a campaign around basic needs and service delivery, expanded their cause to a focused political agenda, and eventually consolidated a support base. South Africa is a country governed by a strong one-party majority, with weak opposition parties. Social movements thus not only represent many marginalized communities by providing a necessary voice, but they also keep a watch on the incumbent African National Congress, ensuring while it is in power that it operates within a democratic context.

Notes

1   United Nations Development Programme (2003), *South Africa Human Development Report 2003: The Challenge of Sustainable Development in South Africa*, Oxford: Oxford University Press.

2   Richard Pithouse (2005), 'The Left in the Slum: the rise of a shack dwellers' movement in Durban, South Africa'. Paper presented at History and African Studies Seminar, 23 November 2005.

3   Trevor Ngwane (2003), 'Sparks in the Township', *New Left Review*, No. 22 (July/August), pp 37–56.

4   Interview with Trevor Ngwane, Anti-Privatization Forum (17 March 2004). SECC Political Committee (2004), 'Ideas on the SA Local Government Election 2005. Soweto Electricity Crisis Committee', unpublished. Johannesburg.

5   Interview with Bongani Lubisi, SECC Organizer (9 March 2005), Soweto.

6   Interview with Virginia Setshedi, Soweto Electricity Crisis Committee (10 March 2004), Johannesburg, founding member of the SECC.

7   Interview with Trevor Ngwane, SECC Organizer (23 May 2006), Soweto.

8   SECC Political Committee (2004), 'Ideas on the SA Local Government Election 2005. Soweto Electricity Crisis Committee', unpublished. Johannesburg.

9   Interview with SECC committee member (23 May 2006), Soweto.

10 Interview with Johannesburg Water representative, March 2005.

11 Ngwane, *op.cit.*

Demba Moussa Dembélé

25
Senegal: Social movements lead the struggle against neoliberalism

The social movements in Senegal have been involved in most of the great mobilizations of people at the subregional, continental and international levels. On the national level, they have been at the head of the struggle against neoliberal policies and contributed to the development of a new citizens' consciousness.

Participation in the large mobilizations

Senegalese social movements, represented by peasant organizations, women's organizations and NGOs, participated in the memorable events of Seattle, in December 1999, on the occasion of the World Trade Organization (WTO) ministerial conference. This was a catalysing experience in mobilizing the Senegalese movements within the alternative world movement that gave birth to the World Social Forum (WSF).

The Senegalese social movements made another major contribution to resistance against the dominant system at the international conference for debt cancellation in Africa and the Third World, the theme of which was 'Africa: from Resistance to Alternatives', held in Dakar in December 2000. Three hundred people came from all over the world, including some thirty African countries. The quality of the participants and their discussions as well as of the resolutions adopted,[1] and the huge mobilization of the population of Dakar during the march closing the conference, all assured it of a success even beyond the expectations of the participants. In this, the Senegalese trade unions played a key role.

Another factor contributing to the success was the great solidarity among the movements of the North and the South, symbolized by the first South/North summit, which brought together, on the fringes of the conference, the movements affiliated to Jubilee South and their partners in the North, all united in their struggle to cancel unconditionally the illegitimate debt of the countries of the South and to abolish the policies of the World Bank and the International Monetary Fund (IMF).

Struggles against neoliberal policies

This conference had a lasting result in that it put the question of the debt of Senegal and of other African countries at the forefront of the concerns of Senegalese social movements. It also opened new horizons for these movements and reinforced their ties with other social movements in the world. This enabled representatives of the Senegalese movements to participate in the first World Social Forum at Porto Alegre in January 2001. The reports made by these representatives and their echoes in the media helped to reinforce the resistance of the social movements to neoliberal policies. This was illustrated by an intensification of the struggle for the cancellation of the debt of Senegal and other African countries, the opposition to the conditionalities of the international financial institutions (IFIs) and above all a radicalization of the struggles against the economic and social policies of the different Senegalese governments.

Opposition to the privatization of certain basic social services such as water and electricity, and to austerity policies, was largely responsible for destabilizing the old 'socialist' power and for its fall in March 2000, during the presidential elections. One of the symbols of these struggles was the successful resistance against the privatization of the electricity company SENELEC (Société Nationale d'Electricité du Sénégal), which had been imposed by the World Bank and the IMF in 1999 but which was cancelled in 2001 by the new government, under the pressure of the unions and public opinion. In spite of this, however, the new liberal authorities tried to return to most of the same policies dictated by the World Bank and the IMF, thus pushing the social movements to stiffen their resistance to its policies. So much so that Senegal has become a veritable social cauldron, with strikes or demonstrations organized almost every week, by workers in the private sector and by state employees, peasant organizations, students and associations of the handicapped.

These social struggles have helped to develop a new citizens' consciousness, as can be seen by the new forms of contestation of public policies that call for 'good governance'. Since 2001 there has been a series of contestations at the local and national level, the aim of which has been to denounce the bad management of the public authorities and to express the people's refusal to suffer in silence the consequences of such management. Thus there have been spontaneous demonstrations in certain districts of Dakar and other urban centres by citizens who are dissatisfied with how their schools or their medical dispensaries are run, with the lack of drinking water or sudden interruptions of the power supply. There have also been more spectacular demonstrations, like the roadblocks – some on the main highways – to call the attention of the authorities and the public to a certain problem and the need to find a rapid solution for it.[2]

Birth of the Senegalese Social Forum (FSS)

The convergence of the struggles carried out on different fronts and the influence of the World Social Forum and the African Social Forum, set up in January 2002 in Bamako (Mali), helped to create the Senegalese Social Forum, which organized its first session in December 2003 in Dakar. Several hundred people took part, including members of trade unions, peasant associations, youth movements, women's associations, NGOs and representatives of several political parties. The main theme of the forum was 'What are the alternatives to the destructive policies of neoliberalism?' The plenaries and workshops provided the opportunity to discuss all the important questions about which the social movements are concerned: youth unemployment, privatizations, increasing living costs, liberalization policies, foreign debts, relationships with the IFI, etcetera.

The theme of the second session of the Senegalese Social Forum was 'The privatization of social services and the withdrawal of the State'. The use of local languages and the holding of the forum in a popular district created a democratic and inclusive space in which ordinary citizens could express themselves in all freedom about their daily problems – problems that have been exacerbated by the privatization or semi-privatization of such essential services as water and health. According to the Declaration that was published at the end of the session:

> The privatizations are based on lies or myths which are presented as irrefutable truths … They have been translated into a sheer selling-off of the national heritage and the control of key sectors of our economy by multinational groups …The participants rejected the privatizations imposed on our country and executed by the governments of Senegal without concern for their disastrous effects on the life of the population of Senegal. They demand a halt to these privatizations and the opening of a genuine national debate on these policies … the termination of all privatization contracts in strategic sectors and their taking over by the State and other public authorities. They declare that endogenous solutions exist at the national, regional and African levels and should always receive priority over those imposed from outside.

One of the main results of this second session of the Senegalese Social Forum has been to put the question of the privatization of public services at the centre of the debates on the economic and social policies of the country. The Senegalese social movements decided to make this question one of the chief themes of the campaign during the general elections, announced for February 2007. Another question that is at the centre of current discussions is that of the free trade agreements, known discreetly as the Economic Partnership Agreements (EPAs), which are currently being negotiated between the European Union and the African countries. The Senegalese social movements are at the forefront in the struggle against these EPAs, particularly because of their foreseeable consequences on agricultural policies in Senegal.

The campaign against the EPAs is being organized by a broad coalition, including the network of peasant organizations and agricultural producers in West Africa (ROPPA) and other peasant organizations and women's organizations, as well as several Senegalese NGOs and NGOs from the North based in Senegal. This coalition is not content with just rejecting the EPAs in their present formulation, but also proposes alternatives that could help Senegal and other countries in West Africa to attain food self-sufficiency, which is a guarantee of food sovereignty.[3]

Strengths and weaknesses

The main strength of the Senegalese social movements lies in the experience they have acquired over several years of struggle and resistance to neoliberal policies. This experience explains why, among other factors, they enjoy credibility in the discussions on economic and social policies. Various parts of the social movement have developed solid links of trust with the population to the extent that they have succeeded in playing an important role in recomposing the social fabric that has been damaged by structural adjustment policies. And lastly, the movements are very diverse in the broad range of their commitment. Indeed there are hardly any fields in which they are not involved, whether at the national, regional or local levels.

Nevertheless they do have a certain number of problems which risk hindering their development and above all weakening their role in the debates on national policies. One of the problems is the imbalance between a few large NGOs, which have many resources and a high profile, and the myriad of organizations, above all in the rural world and on the periphery of the urban centres, whose actions are not so visible as they should be. The former tend to attract attention and resources to the detriment of the grassroots work carried out by the latter. The second problem is linked to the limited resources of the vast majority of the social movements and their dependence on external 'partners'. This tends to limit their autonomy, thus their credibility in the debates on public policy. It is also true that the capacity of analysis of a good number of Senegalese social movements on certain specific questions is limited, if not nonexistent.

The challenges to be taken up

The first challenge is to build on the achievements of the Senegalese social movements and to maintain a high level of mobilization if they are to continue to be an indispensable actor in the debates on public policies. In fact, the great development problems that Senegal faces pose enormous challenges to the social movements, who have to find methods of struggle and mobilization that can galvanize their members. This is the condition on which they can maintain their role as a recognized actor in the development discussions. As these debates are complex, the social movements must improve their analysis capacities so as to be able to contest existing policies and above all propose credible alternatives.

This poses the question of financial means, which condition both their autonomy and their credibility. Dependence on external partners risks certain movements being seen as the intermediaries of the NGOs from the North, whose agenda does not necessarily coincide with that of the local movements. There is another danger, linked with the possibility of being co-opted by certain donors (the European Union, World Bank, etcetera). Finally, the Senegalese social movements must find an appropriate balance between their indispensable unity and the great diversity of their members. The solutions to such problems will condition to a large extent the credibility of the social movements and the level of their involvement in defining and implementing development policies.

Notes

1   Including the 'Manifesto of Dakar' which castigated the neoliberal paradigm and called on the African countries to break with it and opt for endogenous development, with democratic and popular policies and greater cooperation between the countries of the South.

2   Alfred Ignis Ndiaye, 'Les nouveaux acteurs locaux et la démocracie de la bonne gouvernance' in *Mouvements sociaux contemporains à l'échelle mondiale et locale*, Senegal (Dakar) team, June 2006.

3   See, especially, Babacar Ndaw, *Pour une sortie de crise de l'agriculture ouest africaine dans le contexte des négociations commerciales*, Dakar: Réseau des organisations paysannes et des producteurs agricoles de l'Afrique de l'Ouest (ROPPA), June 2006.

IV Asia

Teresa S. Encarnacion Tadem

26
Internationalizing the campaigns against the Asian Development Bank

It was in May 2000, during the 33rd annual conference of the Asian Development Bank (ADB) in Chiang Mai, that global social movements (GSMs) first joined forces with Thai social movements in waging campaigns against the Asian Development Bank. These campaigns have been described as one of the most successful protest movements ever organized against the Bank. As an ADB official admitted, they forced the Bank to really listen to people's demands which would probably not have been achieved through dialogue. Moreover, they resulted in the abolition of the ADB–NGO Coordinator's Office which was replaced with the NGO Coordination Network with greater resources. Some saw this as an acknowledgement of the ADB's need to engage civil society actors.

Among the issues that galvanized the protest actions were the water tax that the ADB wanted to impose; the privatization of social services such as schools and hospitals; and the Bank's Samut Prakarn Waste-water Management Project (SPWMP), which the Klong Dan villagers of Samut Prakarn, among others, claimed was riddled with corruption and environmentally unsound. These issues were brought out in the anti-ADB campaigns in two main venues. One was a parallel conference organized by NGOs under the umbrella of the People's Forum 2000 on the ADB. The other was in the anti-ADB demonstrations led by the People's Network of 38 Organizations consisting mainly of grassroots members. For the People's Forum 2000, the major Thai NGO organizers included the NGO Coordinating Committee on

Development (NGO–COD), Towards Ecological Recovery for Regional Alliance (TERRA) and the Project for Economic Recovery (PER).

Support was forthcoming from international and regional social movements which since the 1970s have been challenging the international financial institutions (IFIs), like the World Bank (WB) and the International Monetary Fund (IMF). But unlike the WB and IMF projects, ADB projects had been basically unchallenged for decades until 1988, when there was a concerted effort among NGOs in the region – among which was the Asian NGO Coalition on Agrarian Reform and Rural Development (ANGOC) – to systematically question ADB projects. Together with the Environmental Policy Institute (now Friends of the Earth–US), ANGOC criticized what it conceived to be the ADB's badly designed and destructive projects. It also noted the absence of dialogue on policy reforms and the need for greater transparency and public accountability (Quizon and Perez-Corral 1995).

For the anti-ADB campaigns in Chiang Mai, international and regional NGOs were drawn in, since the campaigns involved issues that were at the very heart of their advocacy work. The question of corruption in IFI-funded development projects, for example, is the main concern of the Bank for Information Center (BIC) which is based in Washington, and Probe International Canada, while international NGOs whose advocacy is the protection of the environment include Greenpeace Southeast Asia, the International Rivers Network, the Center for International Enviromental Law (CIEL) and Mekong Watch Australia. And Focus on the Global South is one of the international NGOs that have been highly critical of the IFIs' development policy, as epitomized by the neoliberal framework of the ADB's projects. NGOs such as the Society for Environment and Human Development (SEHD) in Bangladesh, and the Citizens' Alliance for Reforms for Efficient and Equitable Development (CREED) in Pakistan, whose countries have been adversely affected by ADB policies and projects, also joined the anti-ADB campaigns in Thailand, as did Japanese NGOs such as Mekong Watch Japan, which were highly critical of how their taxpayers' money was being used by the ADB.

Such broad participation in campaigns like this can also be attributed to the intensification of globalization and the growing strength of IFIs, so that democratization at the local and global levels has become closely intertwined with the domestic situations, as 'unrepresentative decisions on global issues can run counter to democratization within a state and undermine a people's commitment to it' (Boutros Ghali 1993). Thus, it is not surprising that 'during the past decade, one has witnessed the rise of transnational networks, alliances and coalition of diverse socio-political groups chiefly dedicated to the contestation of "globalization" in its various guises' (Colas 2002).

The anti-ADB campaigns were no exception and they provided the basis for these international alliances of NGOs in assisting the Klong Dan villagers and the Thai social movements in their campaign against the SPWMP. Their chief objective was to subject the project to the ADB's inspection officials to determine whether the Bank had complied with its own policies and procedures in processing and implementing the project. They helped by putting pressure on the Thai government and the ADB officials, both locally and internationally, that is, in Washington. A letter-writing campaign was also initiated by the international alliance of social movements challenging the ADB and demanding that it address the issues raised by the Klong Dan villagers. Together with the Thai NGOs, they sent letters to the ADB president calling for the Bank to halt loan disbursements for the SPWMP until an official Bank inspection had been carried out.

Forums on the SPWMP were also held in countries hosting the ADB annual governors' meeting, including the one in Hawaii in 2001. The Klong Dan village leader Dawam Chantarahassadee spoke in an internationally organized NGO forum, at which delegates from the US, Australia and Japan were among the audience. Forums on the SPWMP were also held in Japan to get the attention of the Japanese Ministry of Finance, which funded the project through its Japan Bank for International Cooperation (JBIC). The international alliance of NGOs also assisted the villagers in critiquing the terms of reference the ADB had set up for its Inspection Panel for the SPWMP. All these efforts bore fruit in March 2002 when the Final Report of the Inspection Panel on the project found that there has been noncompliance by the Bank with its policies and procedures in processing and implementation. A year later, in June 2003, the JBIC asked the Thai government for the immediate repayment of 1.6 million baht. The government cancelled its contract with the NVPSKG consortium in February 2003 for breach of contract after handing over some 20 billion baht (Kongrut 2003).

Vinod Raina

27
India: Neoliberalism, caste politics and farmer suicides

Developments over the past year indicate that the hope of ordinary people and social movements that the United Progressive Alliance government would act in their favour was essentially unfounded. Hopes were raised because of the way the UPA came to power after the 2004 general elections. No one had expected that the ruling right-wing National Democratic Alliance coalition, which fought the election with their India Shining campaign, would lose. That they did so signified a decisive rejection of the neoliberal economic policies at the heart of the India Shining campaign. Ordinary people came out with an unequivocal verdict that India might be shining in the pages of *Time,* the *Economist* and the Indian national media, but as far as they were concerned, agricultural debts, bad or inadequate access to education, food and work, forced displacements and corruption had engulfed them all to an unprecedented degree.

At least some of those within or backing the UPA, particularly the left-wing parties, were conscious that people had given it a mandate to tackle these issues. This became evident when a sizeable number of individuals from within social movements, together with intellectuals and academics who support them, were consulted or drafted into committees set up to examine the problems. These included the National Advisory Council, the Central Advisory Board for Education, the Commission for Unorganized Labour, and the National Rural Health Mission. And, within a year of the UPA coming to power, hopes were raised with the passing of the Right to Information Law and the Rural Employment Guarantee Scheme.

But a series of setbacks have now dashed these hopes. Neoliberal interests and sentiments seem to be coming back with a vengeance. Let us take farmer suicides, for example. The Food and Agriculture Minister informed the parliament in late 2006 that some 100,428 farmers had committed suicide since 1993, when the economy was liberalized and privatized in India. That is a truly astonishing figure. On the very day when the prime minister was visiting Vidharbha, one of the farmer suicide areas in Maharashtra state, three suicides took place in the vicinity; more have occurred even after his announcement of a relief package for farmers.

The dead farmers are shouting loud and clear that relief packages are not what they need, but systemic and structural agricultural economy laws and schemes that include credit, pricing and agricultural inputs, rather than measures necessitated by World Trade Organization regulations. Small wonder, therefore, that the Doha Round at the WTO has collapsed because, apart from other factors, India refused to negotiate on agriculture: the farmer suicides have ensured that, at least.

However, the National Planning Commission and the Finance Ministry, headed by diehard neoliberal economists, with support from the prime minister, himself the economist who planned the opening up of the Indian economy, stand firmly against any systemic and structural changes in favour of farmers, for they believe in globalized agriculture. So how long will the position on agriculture adopted by India at the recent WTO meeting at Geneva be maintained?

The same could be said about infrastructure development. India has a huge population that depends on common property resources, using land, water, forests and other natural resources for their subsistence. Once they are dispossessed of these, they have no alternatives to ensure their survival. Dam and road building, airports, urbanization, mining, game parks and sanctuaries, which require large-scale displacement, result in the deprivation and further marginalization of large numbers of people.

A celebrated example of struggle on such issues is the Narmada Bachao Andolan (NBA, the Save the Narmada Movement), composed of people being displaced by the dams on the Narmada river. With the intervention of the Supreme Court, a law established that the height of the forthcoming Sardar Sarovar dam would be increased only after the displaced had been rehabilitated. With strong evidence that most of those displaced from the previous construction had not been rehabilitated, the NBA approached the government to disallow further construction, which had been authorized in March 2006. Their request was ignored by the government, forcing the NBA to go on a hunger strike and mount a sit-in in Delhi that attracted unprecedented support, also from parties on the left, as well as attention in the media.

The government then sent a committee of three central ministers to verify the claims of the oustees. This committee endorsed the evidence of the protestors and requested the prime minister to take action. But he ducked responsibility and asked the courts to intervene. In an unprecedented move, the Supreme Court violated its own earlier judgement, dismissed the report of the three ministers as bordering on the frivolous, and allowed construction to go ahead. This decision of the court and the prime minister's stance have completely alienated large numbers of people and their movements who are fighting for social justice in relation to forced displacements all over the country.

While the Narmada protests were still simmering, a most unusual protest took over the streets of Delhi. The protagonists were not the *dalits,* the *adivasis* or the displaced people, but middle-class medical students. They were protesting because the government had announced its intention of increasing the reserved places in higher education institutions for *dalits* and other backward castes (OBCs) by 27 per cent, a move that had the backing of the national parliament. All hell broke out. The impact would be felt mostly by medical postgraduates, and so upper-caste and middle-class medical students, numbering a few thousand, became frontline heroes of the neoliberal media and corporate intellectuals who asserted that, by compromising 'merit' through caste-based reservations, there would be an erosion of the global edge of the Indian workforce in information technology, management and BPO (business process outsourcing).

Nothing has shown up so sharply the caste and class divisions within Indian society as this reservation issue, which also exposed the double standards of the neoliberals. Only a month previously they had been lamenting the use of street protests by the Bhopal gas victims and the Narmada displaced, who were parked in Delhi for nearly a month. According to the neoliberals, the marginalized were adversely affecting city life and reducing efficiency, but all that talk vanished when their own tribe took to the streets. They were eulogized by the same media and corporate interests. As a consequence, sharp divisions in the ruling UPA have been exposed, while the reservation issue is far from solved.

Even the two victories of the social movements mentioned earlier, the passing of the Rural Employment Guarantee Act (REGA) and the Right to Information Act (RTI), turned sour. The first is being implemented only falteringly, while the second has been completely diluted. It could have served as a strong deterrent against the rampant corruption; it could have helped to assign responsibility and demand accountability from individuals in the government, as it gave the right to a petitioner to access most government files and data. Scared stiff of being made accountable by the notes of officers being made public, the bureaucracy waged a secret war to have their notes removed from the dispositions of the act, so that individual officers' actions would not become known. And the government, to the anger and disgust of the movements, passed an amendment to this effect. This is currently being challenged through protests all over India.

To top all the disaffection between the social movements and the government, the Right to Education Bill, that was to be introduced in parliament as a consequence of the 86th amendment passed by parliament to give the right to education to 6–14-year-olds, is now planned to be dropped as central legislation and relegated to each state. Years of campaigning had gone into pressuring the parliament to pass the 86th amendment, but the central government has quietly concluded that a constitutionally backed right to education would create unnecessary constraints on governmental expenditure and would not be in the interests of the neoliberal economy.

The UPA government depends upon the support of the left-wing parties. However, its recent actions, which include the Indo–US nuclear deal, the privatization of airports and the selling off of public sector assets, have brought ideological cleavages into the open. The social movements are now discovering the neoliberal domination within the UPA and are openly hostile. Not only is the relationship between the movements and the government a serious cause for worry; there is now, for the first time, speculation about the continuing existence of the UPA. With the neoliberal religious fundamentalist right-wing opposition waiting in the wings, the choice for the people and their movements is literally between the frying pan and the fire.

Chantana Banpasirchote and Uchane Cheangsan

28
The tyranny of the majority and the *coup d'état* in Thailand

In September 2006 a military *coup d'état* in Thailand overturned 'Thaksinocracy',[1] as the regime run by Prime Minister Thaksin had come to be called. Thaksin had been democratically re-elected in 2005. But the populist and authoritarian style of his administration, together with its neoliberal orientations, mobilized the social and democratic movements of the country.

Since Thaksinocracy was confirmed, with the elections of 2005, the socio-political scene in Thailand has been very confused and there has been a regression of democracy. Already in 2003, only two years after the start of the first Thaksin administration, part of Thai public opinion had begun to be concerned by the increasing restriction of democratic liberties. In fact the regime was moving towards an 'authoritarian democracy' (Thitinan Pongsudhirak 2003, 277–90) in which the prime minister, as CEO of Thailand, was fixing all the rules of the game. But it was only gradually that the political tensions created by Thaksin-ocracy began to mature, as the government, although it resorted to anti-democratic measures, had itself been democratically elected. And, above all, Thaksin's populist economic policies – funds allocated to the peasants, health coverage of 30 bahts per family – and his tough anti-drug policy[2] had gained him the support of a large section of the population who were ready to exchange certain democratic values for governmental stability and concrete economic returns. This is how Thaksin was able to build 'his' representative democracy, combining State nationalism and entrepreneurial management.

The military *coup* put an end to the 'reign' of this former business-man. The putsch was, however, ambiguous because it was popular and it took place amidst strong political tensions between the detractors and the partisans of Thaksin and against a background of increasing discontent among the middle classes of Bangkok, infuriated by the repeated corruption scandals. Thaksin and his entourage had been mixed up in a number of business affairs since 2001 and the conflicts of interest were so common within his administration that the expression 'corruption politics' was invented to describe his style of management.

Social movements up against the Thaksin government

Thaksin's Party, the Thai Rak Thai (TRT, Thais Love Thais), was the first party to win democratic elections according to the 1997 constitution. With former student militants from the democratization movements of 1973 and 1976 in certain key posts, relationships between the government and the popular movements – the most well known being the Assembly of the Poor[3] – got off to a good start. The movements thus expected to have a voice in decision making, all the more so because the leading role they had played in democratizing the Thai political system gave it a distinctly participatory flavour.

Contrary to all expectations, once the popularity of the new government was established thanks to its populist policies, its relationships with the social movement rapidly deteriorated, to the point that any negotiation became impossible. Emboldened by the governmental stability provided by the 1997 constitution, by his own possessions in the tele-communications field, and by the business community, the prime minister had no hesitation in manipulating the political agenda to give maximum powers to the elected representatives (the law of the majority) and to marginalize social movements, transforming citizens into passive spectators in the political arena. This authoritarian way of governing had a number of consequences for the relationships between the State and civil society.

First of all the NGOs who were acting as intermediaries of the communities were isolated and accused of having no legitimacy to represent the people. The TRT went so far as to call them the 'courtiers of poverty'. Paradoxically, this helped the organizations and popular networks to affirm their independence. The relationships between the

NGOs and the popular organizations became clearer: in the movements, the NGOs limited themselves to a role of technical support and did not involve themselves in the organization and leadership of the communities.

Then the populist policies divided the popular movements. The university personality Somkiat Pongpaiboon, an important figure in the social movements, adopted the method used by the TRT to rally the poor peasants through the technique of 'direct selling', at the end of which these peasants had become completely dependent on governmental funds and the head of State. The rural world was, as a result, considerably weakened.

And finally, by demonizing the progressive sectors of civil society, the State reawakened some of the most conservative tendencies. Two personalities who were linked to the bloody *coup d'état* of 6 October 1976, Dusir Siriwan and Samak Sutraravei, made a spectacular return to the public arena through the media. Still more striking, an informal network called the Anti-NGO Club was created to denounce the activities of the NGOs and to demand that they be more strictly regulated. This development should be seen as a setback to the dominant NGO strategy: by being henceforth essentially oriented toward the State and neglecting civic education and communication with the rest of society, they lost the trust of the general public.

The poor peasants

After having withdrawn from the scene for nearly two years following the repression of their last demonstration, the members of the Assembly of the Poor set up a permanent people's committee to monitor the populist policies of the government. Their strategy changed: they abandoned the large-scale demonstrations to which they had treated the inhabitants of Bangkok and instead organized public forums to raise the awareness of the population. That did not however prevent them from organizing smaller demonstrations, one in front of parliament (from 15 to 17 March 2005) and the other at the Ministry of Agriculture (from 20 to 25 February 2006). The declining popularity of the government made it possible for these movements to return to the negotiating table. They cleverly profited from the situation to force the cabinet to issue a decree blocking two projects for dam construction, one at Klongklai in the province of Nakornsrithammarat and the other at Ruproh in the province of Chumporn.

By choosing to negotiate with the Thaksin government, the Farmers' Debt Network of Thailand too obtained a number of concessions. This network, composed of indebted peasants, acted like an interest group dealing direct with the government, using pressure, lobbying and negotiation, by turns. In particular, they pushed the government into applying the act on farmer rehabilitation and the development fund, adopted in 1999 to help peasants manage their debts. In August 2006 the fund bought nearly 400 debts owed by peasants to commercial banks, for a total of 20 million bahts. This measure was then to be extended to 45,000 peasants, covering 6 billion bahts of debt (Than Settakit 2006).

Opposition to neoliberalism: privatization and free trade treaties

Although privatization was one of the main issues of the elections of 2001 and the TRT regularly played the economic nationalism game, as well as claiming to champion the rights of workers and the interests of consumers, none of the elected representatives kept their promises in this field. This is the reason why the opposition to privatization became the hobbyhorse of the trade-union movement, particularly in the public enterprises, during the two Thaksin governments. The most important campaign was the one concerning the state enterprise EGAT (Electricity Generating Authority of Thailand), which the Thaksin government was accused of wanting to privatize, not to improve its efficiency but to raise its share value. In 2004, large demonstrations, with the participation of several thousands of workers in the public enterprises, demanded a halt to the privatization of public enterprises, the abolition of the law on the state enterprises, and a referendum on the question of privatization.

In 2005 it was the consumer movement, organized by the consumer foundation and the federation of consumer organizations, that took up the baton. Its approach and arguments being different from those of the workers, and more accepted by the general public, it succeeded in creating a broader backing for the struggle against privatization. The coalition of various social sectors and the cooperation between civil society and part of the political society — the Senate — finally bore fruit in 2006 when the administrative tribunal brought by the foundations concluded that there had been irregularities in the privatization of EGAT and that the enterprise had to be withdrawn from the stock exchange.

But it was the movement against the free trade treaty that seemed to be the best organized and the most sophisticated. A free trade observatory, FTA Watch, was established to coordinate the organizations working on the impact of free trade on trade and development. These included the network of HIV positive victims, the networks of slum dwellers in four regions, the network for an alternative agriculture, the Northern peasant federation, the network of consumers, and student organizations.

On 10 January 2006, during the trade negotiations between Thailand and the United States at Chiang Mai, the demonstrations organized by this broad network attracted over 8,000 participants, forcing the negotiators to interrupt their discussions and to leave the hotel where they had been meeting. The main concern of the network was to reject commercially unacceptable conditions on the question of patents, particularly patents on living organisms (FTA Watch 2005). In addition the dissolution of parliament on 24 February 2006, the umpteenth attempt of Thaksin to resolve the political crisis, helped to postpone the trade negotiations with the United States and Japan.

Human rights and democracy

A number of important initiatives have been launched by Thai civil society to deal with the human rights violations committed in the war on drugs and the 'pacification' campaign of the Muslim south.[4] The defence of human rights and that of the media are relatively recent issues, but they have developed rapidly . The disappearance of Somchai Neelapaijit, President of the Association of Muslim Jurists and Vice-President of the Human Rights Committee of the Association of Jurists of Thailand, made people more aware of the role of human rights militants and the risks they ran. As a response to the injustices committed against Muslims of Malay origin and a certain number of suspect disappearances, an informal working group on 'justice for peace' was set up at the beginning of 2006 to investigate legal procedures. In light of the threats hanging over Thai democracy, recent actions looking into legal procedures and mechanisms can be considered a democratic advance. Victims of injustice who would once have had to suffer in silence are now reacting and having their cases taken up.

But the campaign that has had the highest visibility has been the anti-Thaksin campaign. It was by selling his shares in the telecommunications Shin Corp to the Temasek company of Singapore that Thaksin committed his most serious mistake, because that unified all his opponents. That was in fact what made the 'historic' democratic movement, the Campaign for Popular Democracy (CPD),[5] decide to join the anti-Thaksin movement which had been led for several months by the controversial journalist Sondhi Limthongkul, who demanded that the monarchy intervene to depose Thaksin.

The resulting Alliance of People for Democracy was socially homogeneous, as it was composed mainly of members of the middle classes of Bangkok, but it was politically multifarious, as it brought together royalist militants and progressives in the same demonstrations. The compromise worked out between the CPD and the troops of Sondhi to get the monarchy to intervene, and the *coup d'état* that followed, gave rise to a new debate within the democratic forces, concerning the relations between means and ends. Was it not astonishing that some of the most eminent democrats chose to break with the democratic order in the hope of a better democracy?[6]

Conclusion

The putsch of 19 September 2006, in a nation divided between the partisans and the enemies of Thaksin, has delivered Thai democracy to its own demons. The unthinkable has happened again and, more than ever before, it is necessary to accept the complexity of politics in Thailand. The dilemmas of the *coup*, of the tyranny of the majority and of the role of the monarchy will probably not have an immediate impact on the daily activities of the social movements. But they weigh heavy in terms of consequences for the future. To overcome these confusions and paradoxes, what is needed is a collective effort to understand the nature of the Thai social movements, their relationships with the State and their potential in achieving the rights and aspirations of the population.

Notes

1 Thaksin Shinawatra was elected in 2001 and re-elected in 2005, but then deposed by the military on 19 September 2006.
2 The anti-drug policies of the government brought about 2,500 extra-judicial executions.
3 The Assembly of the Poor is a coalition of peoples' organizations together with the non-governmental organizations who are working with the under-privileged. The coalition was formed in 1995 to build up a new identity for the 'poor' and to make their voice heard. Among others, the movement against dams has been particularly active within the Assembly (Suthy Prasartset 2004).
4 The uprising in the Muslim south of Thailand is a separatist campaign concentrated in three small provinces where the population is of Malay origin (Pattani, Narathiwat and Yala). Since January 2004 and the martial law decreed by the Thaksin government, the region has entered into a cycle of violence, fed both by the insurgents and the army forces supposed to be restoring calm.
5 The Campign for Popular Democracy is a network of militant students, trade unions, NGOs and professional associations that was created in 1975 and reactivated after the 1991 *coup d'état*. It played a key role in mobilizing the population, which led to the adoption of a democratic constitution in 1997.

Dai Jinhua

29
China: The new ways of resistance

It is indeed a paradox that China, the last socialist country with a communist party in power, is at the forefront of capitalism, as it undoubtedly is.

The problems common to the globalized world – accelerating polarization between rich and poor, astounding levels of corruption in bureaucracy, massive but often hidden unemployment, unprecedented internal migration and colonization, urban expansion and rural deterioration – become particularly acute in China because of the sheer size of its population.

While China has achieved spectacularly rapid economic growth (or, more precisely, GDP growth), as well as a mushrooming of mega-cities, over the past decade, inequality in the country has reached unacceptable levels.

It is true that, during the Mao Zedong era (1950s to 1970s), there were various structures of political privileges, differentiation in social strata and, in particular, an urban–rural divide. However, the elimination of classes was a genuine social reality of those times. In contrast, the two decades around the turn of the millennium have been characterized by acute class differentiation and the re-legitimization of a class society.

We shall not dwell upon the absurdity of such developments when the ruling regime is run by the communist party and a socialist government. What makes matters considerably worse is that this huge inconsistency means that the intellectual resources available to oppose these developments are woefully inadequate, as are the real possibilities for resistance. This undoubtedly has to do with the legacies and liabilities of the social realities and the intellectual resources inherited from the country's socialist history.

The historical memories and discourses of the 1950s to 1970s are considered to be liabilities in that a majority of the population in those times did indeed suffer various degrees of deprivation during a comprehensive urbanization process, while China experienced external blockade and isolation, which was accompanied by one stormy 'mass movement' after another within the country.

Then the critical discourses of Chinese intellectuals during the last two decades of the twentieth century, as they reviewed the socialist system under Mao, gradually came to dominate the mainstream discourse in the twenty-first century. When this critical discourse did not have the socialist system as its support or its target, it became the leading force in concealing the complexities of history, as well as in demonizing socialist memories.

Hence, on the one hand there is a continuing vicious, almost unrestrained process of polarization between rich and poor, and, on the other, disorientation and helplessness, due to a total rejection of the historical tradition of socialism. And, as a result of capitalist development, the grassroots organizations that had previously existed under the socialist system have gradually disintegrated or become paralysed. Subaltern masses who have once again been thrown into *capitalisme sauvage* with virtually no social welfare, have been forced to seek ways to rescue themselves.

At the beginning of the new millennium, in contrast to the China of hustling, prospering mega-cities, a different, almost invisible China began to develop. Confronted by the iniquitous realities, some intellectuals have begun to turn to the left. And, while making a critique of global capitalization, they also consider alternative paths for today's China. Under their influence and inspiration, and also as a result of the pressure for jobs by a massive, but unseen army of the unemployed, differences among the young student groups have started to emerge. The more radical have joined with the intellectuals to form the 'new left'.

However, this Chinese new left has no direct linkages to the new left movements in the UK and Europe during the 1950s and 1960s. They are known as the 'new' left because they represent a rescue of leftist criticism and resistance from the grip of the communist party that is in power. They also attempt to go beyond Cold War logic and rethink and practise alternatives for a different world.

The most important theoretical and practical issues confronting this new left is not only the repositioning of China in the global context, but also the redefinition of the nature of Chinese society and the new class structure. This means they must tackle head on the historical liabilities of the socialist era, which must first be liquidated if they are to inherit the valuable historical legacies.

Thus the greatest challenge facing the new left is how to rethink the problems of socialist practice in the second half of the twentieth century and understand how that practice harmed and deprived the people in general and in particular the peasants, so that this will no longer be a theme for discussion monopolized by mainstream, right-wing positions. It is also the key to redeploying the historical legacies of socialism so that they become new resources for social mobilization. This is the past of the future, this is the future of history.

At the present time, the 'rural reconstruction movement' that is taking place is of great importance. It is significant because it directly confronts not only the subsistence problems of the 900 million rural population, but also how the globalization process inevitably brings about massive migration from the rural to the urban areas, the international and domestic exploitation of the peasants, and increasing illegal occupations and expropriation of their land – among numerous other problems. It is significant also because the movement tries to represent and search for a social being, a social organization and a value structure outside capitalist modernization. It endeavours to redefine and practise, in a new urban–rural relationship, new forms of livelihood, production and consumption, as well as re-establishing social organizations and networks with peasants as the key subjects, based on the village communities of traditional China and the grassroots social organizations of the Mao Zedong era.

Since 2004 another important alternative social practice in China has been people's active engagement in the '1,000 Women for the Nobel Peace Prize 2005', a global project initiated by Dr Gaby Vermot. The Chinese organizers participate in this project because they understand that such activities, taking place in various regions across the world, reveal 'another world', not only of women, but also of the increasingly vast number of subordinated people – and reveal not only resistance but also creativity in places where modernization formulas have become bankrupt or totally lost. Globally, gender issues have long been much more than issues of secondary significance: they are interlinked with other fundamental issues and have always been a practical force for creating another world and another logic.

The Chinese organizers are also engaged in this project because they hope to rethink and reveal the value of gender issues as a resource for global alternative practices. They hope to uncover the blind spots and mistakes of socialist, leftist and resistance movements in the past.

It is felt that, in order to dispel the gloom of the global 'Great Failure' of the twentieth century, in order to get rid of the impasse experienced by resistance theories and practices, gender issues can offer insights – and not only on 'women's issues' or on a very visible 'vulnerable sector'. To call up another world means to evoke a new logic, a new language, new organization and new practice. Elements are already there in the creativity of invisible grassroots women in their struggle for survival.

In China the Nobel Peace Prize activities have grassroots women as their principal subject, as they endeavour to foster a network of women's alternative social practices from various regions and in different fields of work. Whether or not the project wins the Nobel Prize is not the main issue. Rather the concern is to demonstrate how the resistance and alternative practices of over 100 women will not only reveal all the suffering concealed by the mainstream media but also redefine war and peace, daily life, and a logic beyond modernization.

The concern is to see how the linkages among the 'peace women' can shape social networks that are different from the conventional ones and to find out how such activities can provide webs and linkages among the pockets of grassroots self-help in their resistance to major forces. In such actions, the effort is to reflect on the significance of feminism for the Third World and, at the same time, to rethink, question and construct new historical subjects and allies for resistance.

Jean-Marc Regnault and Tamatoa Bambridge

30
State and civil society
in the South Pacific

Western thinkers have opposed 'civil or political society' to paternal authority or the natural state. They consider that society as such could not exist in ancient societies because a person is not perceived as an individual in the modern sense: as original freedom and the basis for socialization. Rousseau, Tocqueville and Habermas all agree that modern societies create two kinds of public space: the State, and civil society. In the first, individuals agree to confer their freedom to a sovereign who guarantees the freedom of one and all, while, in the second, individuals are the masters of their private interests. This equality – 'one individual has the same worth as another', which is more symbolic than real – constitutes one of the values of Western societies.

In the islands of the South Pacific, the bases of this philosophy of history are challenged in at least three ways by fieldwork and studies that re-examine the epistemological foundations on which the construction of states and civil societies[1] are based and hence Western history is relativized.[2]

In the first place, traditional societies do not confine individuals within a community straitjacket.[3] R. Firth (1965) in Tokopia, P. Ottino (1972) in Rangiroa, M. Naepels (1998) in New Caledonia have shown that the system of family relationships strongly promotes the autonomy of individual decisions. This individual liberty explains the maintenance of traditional organization and, on the other hand, certain changes in the social structure.

Second, the opposition between ancient and modern has given way to an analysis of dialogical processes. The social organization of clans, chieftainships, extended families is studied in colonial contexts, in relationship to religious influences, globalization and to the usage of the new information and communication technologies. Traditional societies are seen, according to Michel Foucault's perspective, as a social construction *within* modernity.

And, third, numerous studies analyse all the horizontal memberships of an individual (social class, age, religious affiliation, clan), as well as vertical ones (membership of a genealogical network, of a traditional statutory hierarchy) and identify a host of memberships and the contradictions they entail. Such studies suggest societies that are evolving fast, rather than being static.[4]

From this starting point of outlining the problematics, two main questions emerge concerning the State and civil society in the islands: on what foundations is the State constructed and how do societies and states relate to each other, given the mobility of the Oceanic peoples?

A pluralist rather than a unitary State

In *La Société contre l'État* ('Society versus the State'), Pierre Clastres reveals the fallacy of the claims that a State is emerging in societies that are traditionally plural. In the Pacific, a formula such as 'societies in the State' (Wittersheim 2006), *à propos* Vanuatu, is a good example of the need to reconsider the history of the Pacific societies in their problematic relationships with the State.

In the Pacific Ocean, as in Africa and Asia, the State appeared as an external support, first for the missionaries and then for colonialism. For this reason, the State administration has been strongly fought against, as it symbolized an insupportable domination rather than a contract.

Under colonialism, then with independence (in the 1960s), the State institution was integrated into the social organization. But, in contrast to the function that is expected of it in Western societies, the islanders do not demand that the State has a monopoly of legitimate violence. This Weberian monopoly is even contested. Other institutions, traditional and customary, assure the individual of a certain legal security. The villages, the chieftainships and family groupings combine to play roles traditionally left to the State: social welfare, land tenure, food security, etcetera. Most of the constitutions of the island states have included custom as a source of law.

The French constitution itself recognizes the 'personal status' (Article 75 in 1958) and the overseas territory status of Wallis and Futuna recognizes custom, conferring on it part of legal procedures. The work on the anthropology of law carried out in Fiji, Tonga, Samoa, Vanuatu and French Polynesia distinguishes official customs from non-official ones.[5] The former, established by the State, have been given a pounding by the social groups who continue to evolve their customs, thus confirming the absence of a State monopoly over the legal security of citizens. In Samoa, Vanuatu and Papua New Guinea, chieftainships assume many more prerogatives than the State as regards the legal security of citizens.

A deep spiritual link with the invisible world of gods and ancestors coexists with Christian religions, producing numerous syncretic and dialogical processes. An individual is not perceived by these societies as original freedom and a new foundation for socialization, as in Western societies. An individual is seen as belonging to a genealogical chain, a member of a network for a very dense, multiform and multi-centred family relationship.[6]

These characteristics of plural agency among State, customary and social institutions have a bearing on what is meant by civil society.

A plural civil society

In the West, the symbolic equality between individuals makes it possible to build horizontal relationships between groups in relation to social problems. Society mobilizes, sometimes against the State, sometimes to denounce a situation that is judged unacceptable or inegalitarian.

In Oceania, a challenge to aristocratic principles is not considered essential.[7] Public opinion seems more concerned with the lack of change among the aristocracy. If democracy in the Western sense has gained ground, it is above all due to the pressure of foreign nations (especially France, the USA and Australia) and the trading of international assistance for democracy.[8] The succession of the old *ariki nui* (Tupou IV) of Tonga, of the Wallis islands (Lavelua), of Samoa (Tui o Manu'a Tele ma Samoa) and of the Maori (Arikinui Te Atairangikaahu) indicates less the end of a system than the beginning of a new era for other families, chieftainships or clans, competing for access to the throne.

It is important to understand the multitude of horizontal and vertical references and memberships. Since the 1950s, the islands have been experiencing considerable population movements. More than half of the Tongans, Samoans and people from Tokelau live in New Zealand, Australia and the United States. In French Polynesia, two-thirds of the population of the 120 islands are concentrated in Tahiti. Vanuatu and the Solomon Islands have experienced similar population movements. People from Wallis and Futuna are more numerous in New Caledonia than in their respective islands. Oceania is the only sea space where there is such a demographic mobility, one that seems to be the rule rather than the exception.

The circular mobility of people over more than 40 million square kilometres has contributed to the emergence of a middle class that is mainly localized on the periphery of the Pacific islands. And it has given rise to specific types of intervention in the public domain. Many public debates about the problems of island society do not take place in the island territories but in Auckland, Fiji and Hawaii.

The strikes and protest marches in Tonga in 2006 against the seizure of the State by the Tongan nobility were mainly prepared by associations based in Auckland.

Professor Albert Wendt attacked colonialism in Samoa in the 1960s. Since the 1990s he has been denouncing the corruption of the chiefs and the way they use power to monopolize the economy. He spoke from Auckland, then from Hawaii, where he now teaches. He speaks from places that are determinant in understanding the echo that his criticisms receive in Oceania intellectual and social circles. Localized criticism takes on the status of regional criticism, which is often relayed through the internet and applied to the Pacific as a whole.

In this context, civil society is certainly not homogeneous. It appears to be de-territorialized: society is no longer confined within circumscribed insular limits. The diaspora not only contribute to the emergence of a counterforce to the State: they also reinforce the plurality of power in their original society and accept specific forms of intervention in the public space.[9] Because of their family ties and the redistribution that they consider is owed to their village or their family, the various diasporas have helped to develop customary ceremonies in their island of origin on a scale and with a frequency that were unknown even in pre-European times.[10]

Finally, in the context of political domination, both the Maoris and the Aborigines have used cultural claims as an effective social tool. The claim for environmental preservation does not stem, as in the West, from the basis of humanism extended to the environment, but on the recognition of the autochthonous rights and obligations when applying the Waitangi treaty imposed in 1840.

In this context of the mobility of populations and the anchorage of Oceanic states, the opposition between 'micro territorialized states' and deterritorialized civil society makes sense only if one takes into account the actions of individuals and groups to maintain the pluralism of their society and of their countries, as well as the development of their networks. To take up and modify the formula of Clastres, the society is the State to the extent that it helps to maintain the pluralism of Oceanic societies.

Australia, now a superpower, has become the 'policeman of Oceania', under the pressure of George Bush, and it is replacing the power of the Pacific states, who do not look on this intrusion with a favourable eye, as indeed nor do their societies. The disorders of the last few years[11] are no doubt due to the fact that the Australians are no longer indifferent to their backyard. New developments may put into question existing analyses on the relationships between States and societies.

Notes

1   See, especially, the series of the Pacific Epistemologies Conferences, the most recent of which was held at the University of the South Pacific in Fiji, 3–7 July 2006.
2   See Chiba (1993); Capeller and Kitamura (1998).
3   Cohen (1994); Sahlins (2000); Hau'ofa (2000); Hooper (2000); Belgrave et al (2005).
4   See, especially, Hau'ofa (2000); Hooper (2000); Belgrave et al (2005).
5   See, especially, Larmour (1997); Bambridge (forthcoming).
6   See Bonnemaison (1985, 1992).
7   See the panorama presented by Crocombe (1992, 1995).
8   See Huffer et al. (2000).
9   Here taken as the intermediary space between the State and society in the Habermasian sense.

10   This sometimes poses new problems: how can one remain chief far from one's island and one's people? See Tui Atua Tupua Tamasese Taisi Tupuola Tufuga Efi (2004).

11   Regnault (2005).

31
Malaysia: Militants confront repression

The Malaysian Socialist Party (PSM) was formed in the mid-1990s and in 1998 it applied for registration as a political party. The application was rejected and the PSM has continued to fight for legal recognition as a party. 'We have taken the minister to court. We are still waiting for the hearing of the appeal,' party leader V. Selvam explained. This restricts the PSM's activity, as 'only registered political parties can contest elections', Selvam said. 'The law does not permit us to work at all, actually. But despite that, we have been working and will continue to work. Freedom of association is guaranteed by the constitution but in practice it does not exist.'

The party works among 'workers, the trade unions, young people, students, urban pioneers (squatters), plantation workers, and the peasantry', Selvam says. The biggest problem confronting the urban pioneers is housing. 'They are forcibly evicted and their houses are demolished. Where they are offered alternative housing, the payments are a bit steep compared to their income. ... The urban pioneers have been campaigning to stop forced evictions. There is a campaign to provide them with decent housing. Some of them have campaigned to keep their land and houses.'

Selvam also described the marginalization of plantation workers. 'The plantations were created in the British colonial period, over a hundred years ago. The workers have lived and worked on the plantations for three generations or more. Their pay is very low, even though they have a union ... The plantations sit on prime land, which is being sold for redevelopment. Plantation workers are being thrown out of their jobs and their houses. At times, the workers are paid a redundancy package for the loss of their jobs, but not for the loss of their houses. The struggle is for alternative housing and also for a decent, fair compensation package and redundancy package.' These struggles have led to some victories for the workers.

Malaysian trade unions are 'pretty weak', according to Selvam, who is a member of the general council of the Malaysian Trade-Union Congress. 'The Trade-Unions Act does not allow sufficient room for unions to function. Trade unions have to be registered first with the Registrar of Trade Unions, and then they have to demand recognition from employers.' Employers often refer the case back to the registrar, where it is stalled. 'The workers have been frustrated by recognition claims pending for years. When recognition eventually comes, it comes too late. By this time the union has lost steam, and many workers have left the workplace. The union does not have sufficient strength to continue with negotiations in an effective way. The percentage of workers in trade unions today is less than 10 per cent. 'We have been campaigning for the laws to be repealed by the government to allow for automatic recognition. The government has been dragging its feet.'

The PSM has also been campaigning with NGOs about continued environmental destruction. Selvam identified logging in East Malaysia and river pollution as two key problems. He also described the PSM's work with 'small-scale farmers who are being displaced due to the rapid development. Often farm land is encroached upon for development purposes, and farmers are not compensated with alternative land to continue their farming activity.'

Students face great repression in Malaysia, according to Selvam. The Universities and University Colleges Act 'does not allow for much student activity. Recently there have been many complaints that student elections were not free. Students were not allowed to campaign. They were not allowed to vote for the parties they wanted.' Students are campaigning to repeal the Act, 'but we are not seeing much progress in this area. Students remain a suppressed lot. When they protest they are thrown out of university.'

Although the PSM is not registered as a party, it fielded four candidates in the last elections – two in federal constituencies and two in state constituencies. 'Since the party is not registered, we were not able to put up candidates under our own party platform. Although in the campaign we pushed our own programme, principles and ideas, we had to either contest as independents or on the party tickets of other parties. In this case we contested, borrowing the party tickets of other opposition parties.' The PSM gained around 30 per cent of the vote. According to Selvam, despite repression of the left, the PSM has also been successful in building mass actions. 'We have been quite effective in mobilizing and organizing the various sectors of society.'

Note

1   This chapter is a slightly edited version of an interview orginally published in *Green Left Weekly* (www.greenleft.org.au), 22 February 2006, on the occasion of the visit of V. Selvam, a leader of the Malaysian Socialist Party (PSM) and general council member of the Malaysian Trade Union Congress, to Melbourne (Australia) early in February 2006 at the invitation of the Socialist Party. *Green Left Weekly*'s Chris Slee spoke to him about current struggles in Malaysia and the work of the PSM.

Jude Lal Fernando

32
Towards a convergence of resistance in Sri Lanka?

In the postcolonial non-Western world the model of the nation-state is considered as the ideal to safeguard the political as well as the economic sovereignty of the decolonized countries. However, the very model of the centralized system of the nation-state (which itself is a colonial product), as well as the interventions of the 'imperial' international financial institutions (in the name of the eradication of poverty and on behalf of development), have aggravated the socio-economic and political crises of these countries. While the dominant model of the nation-state has resulted in protracted ethno-religious conflicts creating millions of refugees, the development models of the international financial institutions (IFIs) have created millions of poor people who live below the poverty line. Sri Lanka, which records 1.2 million Tamil and Muslim refugees (in spite of fifty years as an independent nation-state that claims to guarantee the rights of all communities within a unitary state) and two million families who live below the poverty line (in spite of fifty years of interventions by the World Bank), is a clear example of this crisis situation.[1]

What is most revealing here is how the political crisis that the Sinhala-dominated Sri Lankan state is going through (in the face of the Tamil movement for self-determination and autonomy) is inseparably associated with the economic crisis of the country. This crisis was caused initially by the heavy dependency on colonial economic structures which were based mainly on mercantile capital and later by the continuous structural readjustment programmes of the international financial institutions.

In post-independence Sri Lanka, the majoritarian system of politics (in which the parliament is dominated by an ethno-religious majority) sought to remedy the ever-growing socio-economic grievances of the disgruntled social classes with the discriminatory mechanism of 'robbing Peter to pay Paul'. The Sri Lankan governments after independence launched resettlement schemes for Sinhala peasants in the Tamil areas in the North and East of the country and thereby avoided an uprising of the landless farmers in the Sinhala areas against the landed elite who benefited from the colonial economy. The 'Sinhala Only Act' which made the language of the majority the only official language of the country, while creating space for the Sinhala-educated middle classes to enter into State and public sector employment, deprived the Tamil-speaking employees of their jobs. In seeking to redress the grievances of the Sinhala rural youth with regard to higher education opportunities, the quota of Tamil students was reduced through a scheme of standardization.

As the onslaught of the market economy that began in 1977 continued apace, a massive process of privatization took place under the slogan of 'giving back to people their due economic rights'. As a consequence the 1980s marked the firing of 80,000 public and State sector employees who went on strike, brutal suppression of the insurrection of the rural middle classes (in which over 60,000 were killed) and the militarization of the entire Tamil region in the North and East of the country by the government. It is against this background that the Tamil movement for self-determination and autonomy entered into its militant phase, particularly after anti-Tamil riots in 1983. These riots claimed 3,000 lives and displaced half a million Tamils. The government, following the dictates of the IFIs, cut down farming subsidies and expenditure on welfare, the health and education budget, and promoted foreign investments by loosening tax and labour laws, vowing to the masses that the unitary nation-state would be protected at any cost, without giving in to the Tamil claim to the North and East of the country. The defence budget and the rate of liberalization of the economy increased simultaneously.

The JVP, the Janatha Vimukthi Peramuna (Peoples' Liberation Front), which had led two insurrections, in 1971 and 1979–1989, against colonial and neocolonial economic policies,[2] continued to adhere to the concept of a unitary state despite discrimination against

minorities, particularly the Tamils. During the period beginning 1994–
the JVP began to enter into electoral politics by opposing neoliberal
economic policies in principle, but concretely prioritizing the need to
safeguard the unitary nation-state from the 'threat of Tamil separatism'.
What the movement of the Sinhala rural and urban middle classes who
are led by the JVP have failed to see is the link between their economic
rights and the political rights of the Tamils and other minorities. The
dissatisfied social classes that are endangered by neoliberal economic
policies promoted by the IFIs have become a breeding ground for
religious fundamentalism that envisages a Sinhala Buddhist nation-state.
The emergence of the Sinhala Buddhist political party (JHU) led by the
Buddhist monks during the last decade is a clear reflection of this reality.

By 2001, the heightened military operations of the Sri Lankan government in the Tamil region and the counterattacks by the LTTE
(Liberation Tigers of Tamil Eelam), who lead the Tamil movement, had
destabilized the economy of the country which was increasingly reliant
on foreign investments. It was in this context that the Cease Fire
Agreement (CFA) between the government of Sri Lanka and the LTTE
was signed. A grant of 4.5 billion US dollars was promised by the donor
countries for rehabilitation and reconstruction depending on the
progress of the peace negotiations. Peace was attached to development,
but neither the models of development nor of power devolution were
discussed in depth.

While the centralized State structures remained intact, due to
pressure from the JVP, implementation of neoliberal policies proceeded
further, due to pressure from the 'donors'. Because of legal action taken
by the JVP and JHU parties, the joint humanitarian mechanism that had
been created between the government of Sri Lanka and the LTTE to
reconstruct the tsunami-affected areas had to be stopped. This mechanism was one of the opportunities that could have de-ethnicized the
conflict, paving the way for a common alliance between the two ethnic
groups. Peace negotiations stopped as the US government intervened
by holding a meeting of the donor countries of Sri Lanka in
Washington which excluded the LTTE.

Although the election victory of the nationalist coalition (supported
by the JVP and the JHU) in 2005 has been interpreted as a mandate
given by the people against neoliberal policies, ironically it has also been
interpreted as a mandate to abrogate the CFA and thereby initiate a

militaristic solution to the ethnic conflict. The government, under the current president who heads the nationalist coalition, has so far failed to redress the grievances of the working classes, farmers and fishermen. The promises given to them regarding subsidies and salary hikes, which go against the conditions laid down by the international financial institutions, have not been kept. Instead, the government, under pressure from the JVP and the JHU, have heightened military operations in the Tamil regions, causing the deaths of over 1,000 civilians and displacing 200,000 people within eight months, adding to the death toll of 68,000 lives and 1.2 million refugees during three decades of war. As the pressure from the donor countries on both parties in the conflict to hold on to the CFA and start peace negotiations mounts, the JVP and the JHU are threatening to withdraw their support for the government in the event of any concessions given to the Tamils.

As Jayadeva Uyangoda, head of the department of political science at the University of Colombo, shows,[3] the Tamil movement led by the LTTE has established a 'sub-national state' within the Tamil region. This goes beyond the models of a conventional federalist system.

The Sri Lankan ruling polity find it extremely hard to come to a consensus among themselves with regard to any degree of devolution of power to the Tamil region. The USA, the EU, Norway and Japan are the co-chairs of the committee of the donor countries and the IFIs which oversees the peace process in Sri Lanka. While the EU, Norway and Japan are moved by their economic interests in the island, the moves of the USA are determined by their strategic military interests in South Asia.[4] On the surface it seems as though the government of the nationalist coalition in Sri Lanka chooses to act against the interests of the imperial powers. In reality it is not so. The nationalist coalition, like the previous governments, has relied on US military expertise in its war against the Tamil region while supporting the 'global war on terror'. Not only that, but it continues to suppress the resistance to neoliberal policies.

As reports of the escalation of violence in Sri Lanka increase daily, what is not identified by the progressive forces in the world community is that another round of resistance has begun to emerge from the Sinhala working classes, fishermen and farmers and the Tamil and Muslim communities. Demonstrations by the Tamils and Muslims continue to grow in the Tamil region against the acquisition of land (mostly the paddy fields of the farmers and the beaches of the fishermen), abductions, dis-appearances and killings by the Sri Lankan military. Meanwhile the farmers' organizations, fisheries trade unions, and the public and State sector trade unions who have been let down again, both by the nation-alistic governments (who seek a militaristic solution to the ethnic conflict) and by the IFIs, have begun to protest, shaking the popular base of the government. There is a great potential within these move-ments to form a broader alliance against both neoliberal policies and the Sinhala majoritarian State system.

Even after the government of the nationalist coalition attempted to suppress the major strikes carried out by harbour and railway workers against privatization, calling them 'worse than terrorist attacks', and prohibited the strikes by obtaining court orders, the trade unions have not desisted from protests, and are not giving their support to the idea of war against the Tamils and Muslims. Instead, they have formed a new broader alliance of 52 trade unions that have begun to challenge the government. This is said to be one of the broadest trade-union actions in the country in recent history. More than five political parties in the opposition have threatened the government with a total shutdown of business establishments in Colombo in protest at the continuing abduc-tions of Tamils. The All-Ceylon Fisheries Trade Union has been able to mobilize the masses along the coastal belt demanding a subsidy in the face of rising fuel prices. In their campaign they have also highlighted the rights of their Tamil and Muslim counterparts in the war-torn regions.

The National Farmers' Assembly and the Movement for National Land and Agricultural Reform (MONLAR), through their campaigns, have succeeded in arranging a meeting with the World Bank authorities to state categorically their opposition to structural readjustments by showing how such moves lead to an increase in poverty. They too have incorporated the demands of the Tamil movement by emphasizing the right to land, along with the right to water and livelihood. It is evident that the moves of the 'imperial' global powers, along with their financial institutions, and of those who safeguard the unitary structure of the Sri Lankan state have brought more and more poverty, violence and conflict. Their policies have demonstrably not brought peace and development.

The role of the progressive movements in Sri Lanka needs to be one of forming a common alliance by bringing together the resistance that is emerging from the different sections of society. The present crisis has opened up a historic opportunity to form a common alliance between the various victims of both neoliberal policies and the majority-dominated nation-state. The duty of the progressive political and social movements in the world is to recognize the need to lend both support and concrete solidarity, and in particular to use international platforms to demand an end to government oppression in Sri Lanka.

Notes

1 The Sri Lankan conflict has claimed 68,000 lives and devastated the entire Northern and Eastern regions of the island. Moreover, 50,000 children have been made orphans, 40,000 women widowed and over two million palmyra trees destroyed.

2 The insurrection in 1971 was a clear reflection of the inability of the nation-builders to overcome the colonial economic and education systems that did not suit the needs of the country. The insurrection of 1987–1989 mirrored the socio-economic uncertainties furthered by both economic liberalization and structural readjustments to the economy that constituted, in reality, a new species of colonialism under the guise of capitalist globalization.

3 Jayadeva Uyangoda, 'Peace Watch' in *Polity*, Vol. 1, No. 4, 2004, Colombo: Social Scientists' Association.

4 Of the seven major sea lines of communication in the world, four run through the Indian Ocean. The world's third biggest natural harbour (Trincomalee) is located in Sri Lanka. The area of the harbour is in the predominantly Tamil North and East of the island. For an analysis of the growing geopolitical importance of Sri Lanka in the present global context of the 'politics of energy' and the war on Iraq, see the publications of the *Hiru* Group in Colombo and writings of Dharmaratnam Sivaram in the *Daily Mirror*, Colombo, and on www.tamilnet.com.

Oleh George Junus Aditjondro

33

Indonesia: Paddling through increasingly treacherous and neoliberal waters

Three tendencies have characterized Indonesian social movements during recent years. First, most social movements are politically and ideologically still dominated by middle-class activists. Second, most social movements, and in particular the environmental movement, have focused on the adverse effects of the State's neoliberal policy of favouring large domestic and transnational corporations. Third, these social movements have had to face increasingly hostile forces from within the Indonesian State and society.

Since the capitulation of the Indonesian government to the dictates of the International Monetary Fund (IMF) on 15 January 1998, Suharto and his successors have increasingly opened the Indonesian economy to private interests by selling off many strategic State-owned corporations to domestic and foreign private interests. This has been accompanied by the rapid expansion of private companies owned by – or associated with – members of the ruling elite, including President Soesilo Bambang Yudhoyono, Vice-President Jusuf Kalla, Coordinating Minister for Social Welfare Aburizal Bakrie, and Minister for State Corporations Soegiarto, who owns shares in the Medco Group of businessman-turned-politician Arifin Panigoro. Meanwhile, the President himself is close to Artha Graha, a quasi-military conglomerate led by a young Chinese businessman, Tomy Winata. Interestingly, Bakrie, Panigoro, Kalla and his brother-in-law, Aksa Mahmud, a deputy chairperson of the Indonesian Congress, as well as Tomy Winata, are among the top 40 richest Indonesians, according to *Forbes Asia* (18 September 2006), owning respectively US$ 1.2 billion, US$

815 million, US$ 105 million, US$ 195 million, and US$ 110 million. This concentration of wealth within the ruling elite has given companies close to the authorities the impunity to carry out social and ecological crimes. In East Java, for instance, thousands of villagers have been displaced by an uncontrollable mud flow – covering an area of 180 hectares – from the exploration field of PT Lapindo Brantas. It so happens that Bakrie's family conglomerate and Panigoro's Medco Group are the company's major shareholders. Mud from the explosion, unstoppable since 29 May 2006, with an estimated damage of US$1 billion, will be piped into the Java Sea. Thousands of fishermen from the nearby island of Madura opposed this solution, while residents of the worst-affected Porong district have stoned and set fire to Lapindo Brantas facilities. Hence, at the time of writing, several NGOs are planning to take the company to court, while Greenpeace Indonesia activists have dumped over 640 kilograms of mud in front of the office of Social Welfare Minister Aburizal Bakrie.

Less dramatic yet of no less importance were farmers' protests against the expansion of water-bottling companies, produced by a joint venture of the French transnational corporation Danone, which has encroached on farmers' irrigation water sources. The farmers' protests have not had great success, as their position has been weakened by the new Water Management Law, drafted by USAID-financed experts and legalized by the Indonesian parliament, which has encouraged the privatization of previously public water sources.

Much more visible have been the mass protests by environmentalists and villagers against the construction of large dams. These anti-dam groups have enjoyed much support from the global anti-dam movement (Khagram 2000), especially in Japan and the USA, since the financing and dam-building companies come mainly from those countries. In addition, villagers living close to or under high-voltage power lines linking the power stations with remote industrial centres have begun to be organized by former student activists. On the island of Java, these electromagnetic pollution victims have demanded billions of rupiahs in compensation from the National Electricity Company, PLN. In early 2006, villagers and student activists sewed their mouths in protest against the government's ignorance about the safety, health, and economic well-being of tens of thousands of power-line victims.

In Central Sulawesi, protests against the construction of a 780MW hydropower dam on the Poso River have indirectly led to the execution of three migrant farmers from the island of Flores. Fabianus Tibo, Marinus Riwu, and Dominggus da Silva had sat on death row for five years, being wrongly accused of masterminding communal conflicts in the Poso region. They were executed on 22 September 2006, despite a plea for clemency from Pope Benedict XVI. This unjust and inhuman execution triggered popular protests in Central Sulawesi as well as in the trio's home province, East Nusa Tenggara.

Mass demonstrations, an attack on the provincial police commander, the burning of police offices and cars in a small town in the Poso region, and increasing tensions between Christians and Muslims have led to the deployment of hundreds more soldiers and mobile brigade police forces to Central Sulawesi. Their hidden agenda is, however, to protect the unpopular Poso hydropower project of Vice-President Jusuf Kalla, who had endorsed the execution of the Flores trio.

Another recent example of Indonesia's capitulation to neoliberalism is the opening of the country to the direct marketing of oil and gas products. Shell has currently opened four ultra-modern fuel stations in Jakarta, while the Malaysian oil company has also set up a fuel station in the capital city. In the same neoliberal spirit, the largest oilfield in Java, the Cepu Block, has been granted to ExxonMobil, the US company which is also exhausting the oil and gas fields of Atjeh on the northern tip of Sumatra. Consequently, thousands of villagers in the Cepu, who for two generations have produced crude kerosene from more than five hundred old Dutch wells, are currently on the brink of being evicted.

The capitulation of Indonesia's state oil company, Pertamina, to ExxonMobil, the biggest among Fortune's 500 largest US corporations in 2006, has a sinister background in the mysterious killings of more than 200 Muslim leaders in the Banyuwangi area in East Java in 1998–99. The killings were framed by the authorities as a campaign against black-magic practitioners, called *dukun santet*. In fact, they were to intimidate local leaders who might resist further expropriation of their natural resources. The takeover of land in East Java by big companies using military power was actually the main aim. Bojonegoro is now under the control of ExxonMobil and Monsanto of the USA and PetroChina of Taiwan (Marut 2003).

These companies took over the land in Bojonegoro and its sur-roundings with high-level diplomatic support. The US Consulate

General in Surabaya, East Java, lobbied the local government not to hinder foreign investment initiatives, threatening that this would be against WTO regulations. Meanwhile, during the power vacuum at the grassroots level, George Soros took over the majority of the shares in PT Bentoel, one of the biggest cigarette production companies in East Java, and introduced hybrid tobacco seeds in East Java without any significant resistance from local farmers.

As has been the case in East Java, almost all conflicts in Indonesia after Suharto ended up with new power structures and new structures of control over rich natural resources and investment potential in the country. In other words, regional conflicts reflect a collusion of interests of capital, military factions and paramilitary groups, a new strategy applied by the forces of globalization.

Middle-class activism

Activists originating from the working and 'subaltern' classes, to borrow from Antonio Gramsci, emerged during the last decade of Suharto's rule and increasingly after the end of his dictatorship. They have strengthened the workers', farmers' and indigenous peoples' movements. In the meantime, many young, university-educated people from the middle classes have also joined the movements for the following reasons. First, the judiciary is still controlled by the rich and the powerful, and has not been helpful to workers, farmers and other victims of development seeking to win their cases. Hence, social movements rely mainly on the media and the publishing houses for their advocacy campaigns. Second, the growing number of political parties have not exercised much control over the executive body. In fact, the political parties are controlled by the State's civilian and military arms, in collusion with big business. Third, advocacy work through social movement organizations has the attraction of a counterculture, by offering an alternative to becoming robotic civil servants or joining greedy conglomerates. The emergence of this national counterculture has also been boosted by fellow idealists abroad, who support overseas trips and seminars.

Increasing opposition to their activism has not been a major hindrance for the young middle-class activists. Indeed, facing danger is part of their heroism. The assassination of human rights activist Munir

Said Thalib on board a Garuda flight from Jakarta to Amsterdam on 6 September 2004, has not discouraged them.

Dangers confronting the movements

What are then the major 'dangers' confronting Indonesian social movement activists? There are at least five. First, the continuing domination of the military over the country's bureaucracy and businesses, exercised through the army's territorial structure reaching from Jakarta to the villages. Second, the policy of decentralizing development, which has allowed local government leaders and their military cronies to facilitate the expansion of national business corporations to far-away regions. These local government leaders often act as protectors of national and transnational business interests, since the current law for regional government has empowered local government leaders to approve or reject any investment plan in their regions. Third, the increasing religious intolerance in the country, combined with an increasing ethnic chauvinism triggered by the subdivision of new provinces and districts encouraged by the new regional government law, has created a counter-movement to the social movements fighting for increased justice, human rights and welfare for all citizens, regardless of their race, ethnicity and religion.

Fourth, international funding agencies, working in Indonesia under the conditions set up by the host government as well as by their headquarters in Washington and elsewhere, often impose their masters' wishes on their recipients, which constrain the advocacy work of Indonesian social movement activists. The most blatant example was when two successive US ambassadors put pressure on USAID to cut funding to two Indonesian non-government organizations, namely WALHI (the Indonesian Environmental Forum) and JATAM (the Anti-Mining Advocacy Network), due to their criticism of US mining companies such as Freeport McMoRan and Newmont (Leith 2003: 182–4). Last year, Ford Foundation administrators in Jakarta put pressure on the author (myself) to omit this case from a book on environment and development in Indonesia, to be published by the Foundation to commemorate its fifty years' presence in Indonesia. Refusing to yield to the Foundation's pressure, the author quit from the team of writers of that book.

The last, but not least, danger is the middle-class bias of many social movement activists, whose activism has become a profession. The cases to advocate are numerous and dependent on the media and the publishing houses, so that many issues of social concern often catch the public attention on a very temporary basis.

Teresa S. Encarnacion Tadem

34
Philippine social movements face the challenges of democracy[1]

During the martial law period (1972–86), Philippine social movements led by the mainstream left, namely the Communist Party of the Philippines (CPP), its military arm, the New People's Army (NPA), and its united front organization, the National Democratic Front (NDF), challenged the economic policies pursued by the authoritarian Marcos regime. These development policies were anchored in the development thrust of the International Monetary Fund (IMF) and the World Bank (WB) which espoused an externally propelled capitalist-led development policy characterized by liberalization, foreign invest-ment and an export-oriented thrust as the pillars for economic progress. The lead agent of this development trajectory in the country was the technocracy who had close ties with the IMF/WB and was viewed as an elite corps of experts which had the last word in developing planning (Bello *et al* 1982, 28).

An important aspect cultivated in the ideology of the technocracy is the distaste for politics which is perceived to be 'irrational' and thus anathema to development of 'scientific expertise'. Thus, they welcomed an authoritarian regime as it crushed all forms of political and civil rights and the technocrats enjoyed the unhindered implementation of their policies in the name of economic expediency. Such economic policies, however, increased the poverty in the country and widened the gap between rich and poor. Philippine social movements, there-fore, directed their demonstrations and protest actions not only against the dictator but also against these technocrats who were viewed as the third leg that propped up the martial law regime (the other two being the military and Marcos's relatives and cronies). Protestors would chant 'down with the US/IMF/WB-Marcos dictatorship', with the technocrats seen as the embodiment of IMF/WB policies in the country.

With the advent of the 1986 People Power Revolution, the technocrats were banished and there was hope that civil society players and social movements could now play a role in determining the economic thrust of the post-martial law regime. Section 16 of Article 13 of the 1987 Philippine Constitution even stipulated that 'the right of the people and their organizations to effective and reasonable participation at all levels of social, political and economic decision-making shall not be abridged' (Ariate 2005, 91). Despite such a political milieu, however, there are also factors in the current dispensation which make it difficult for social movement players to intervene in policy making, particularly to counter the adverse effects of globalization.

One factor is the very dominance of the neoliberal ideology among crucial policy-makers. Unlike the martial law period when the liberal market ideology seemed to be the monopoly of the martial law technocrats, this has not been the case during the post-martial law period. What has emerged is that the tenets of neoliberalism are 'not only tenaciously adhered to but also nurtured by like-minded academic experts, think-tanks and consultancy firms working closely with government'[2] (Quinsaat 2005, 32-3). Even the political parties and their members in the Philippine Congress are ardent supporters of privatization and liberalization. Another factor that strengthens the neoliberal ideology is the transnational character of economic policy-making, which means that the Philippine government is 'now more accountable to the institutions of global governance such as the IMF/WB and the World Trade Organization (WTO) alongside the state which exercise hegemony within and over these establishments, than to citizens' (Quinsaat 2005, 33). A third factor that shields the post-martial law technocrats from interference in the decision-making process is the policy environment itself. As pointed out, 'while the law may appear sufficient, even socially progressive, equally important are the openness and hospitality of the politico-administrative environment to civil society participation in policy-making' (Brillantes 1997, 49).

For social movement players, therefore, the challenge posed by a post-martial law regime characterized by an 'illiberal' democracy where politico-economic elites continue to rule called for different strategies to oblige the government to be transparent and accountable with regard to economic decisions. In general, social movements have developed a core group of players who are equipped with the technical capability and know-how to engage the technocracy in particular but also the government in general. An example of such a non-governmental organization is the Freedom from Debt Coalition (FDC) whose intervention at the executive and legislative levels on the issue of debt has led the government to rethink the imposition of a debt cap (Ariate 2006, 13). Another strategy was to form alliances with legislators on the demands of the social movements. The FDC, for example, was able to forge important linkages with independent-minded legislators, a number of whom would eventually craft bills and legislation that in turn would serve as a significant battleground for the cause of debt policy reform (Ariate 2006, 15).

For civil society players who do not possess the technical know-how or organizational capabilities, one recourse has been the formation of alliances with government policy-makers, for example bureaucrats and legislators, as well as with local government officials who would be sympathetic with their needs. Such was the strategy of the Benguet vegetable industry farmers who formed an alliance with local government officials to prevent their livelihood from disappearing because of the onslaught of the importation of cheap vegetables brought about by globalization (Quinsaat 2005, 50). There are legislators too who, although they support the neoliberal ideology in general, succumb to the pressure of public clamour against certain policies. An example was the government's attempt to impose taxes on text messaging. The result was a massive protest campaign, which included Overseas Filipino Workers (OFW), who generally come from the lower classes and who rely on text messaging to connect with their families in the country because long-distance telephone calls are too expensive for them (Molmisa 2005, 177).

There are also bureaucrats occupying key economic positions who are sympathetic to social movement actors. Thus the garment industry, particularly the workers, received support from high-ranking government officials from the Department of Trade and Industry (DTI), the Department of Labor and Employment (DOLE) and the Garments and Textile Export Board (GTEB) regarding the demise of the industry resulting from cheaper garments imported from abroad.

Social movements have also formed alliances with members of the business community, sectors of whom, as happened during the martial law period, were also critical of liberalization policies that impinge on their profits. Similarly, in the post-martial law period they have objected to the policy on trade liberalization, particularly the entry of cheaper, imported products. It is with this sector of the business community that civil society players have formed alliances as can be seen, for example, in the hog industry with the emergence of the Agricultural Sector Alliance of the Philippines (ASAP) in 2001 to protest against the entry of imported meat products into the country which are sold at a lower price than their domestic counterparts (Ariate 2005, 94).

Lastly, social movements have also found allies with international networks and alliances that question the neoliberal ideology. An example of this is 'the Labor Forum Beyond MFA[3] which was formed in early 2003 through the efforts of the International Textile, Garment and Leather Workers' Federation (ITGLFW) Philippines, in order to examine problems experienced by the garment industry in view of the expiry of the MFA and to prepare the workers for the quota phase out...' (Lopez Wui 2006, 133). All these alliances are complemented with protest actions and demonstrations as well as symposiums and advocacy campaigns through newsprint, radio and television, to raise public consciousness on government economic policies that continue to wreak havoc on the lives of the majority.

The experience, therefore, of Philippine social movements in challenging the neoliberal ideology in a period of democracy reveals that, although the martial law regime was more repressive than the current regime, elite democracy coupled with globalization nevertheless creates obstacles that block participation in economic decision making. However, social movement actors have exploited opportunities in the form of alliances, particularly with key decision-makers, to challenge the dominant paradigm which continues to perpetuate poverty and socio-economic inequalities in Philippine society.

Notes

1   For further details, see Teresa Encarnacion Tadem, 2005, 'The Philippine Technocracy and US-led Capitalism' in Shiraishi Takashi and Patrico N.

Abinales, eds, *After the Crisis: Hegemony, Technocracy and Governance in Southeast Asia*, Japan: Kyoto University Press and Trans Pacific Press, pp. 85–104.

2   The University of the Philippines School of Economics, for example, is perceived as a bastion of neoliberal academics. As for the think-tanks, the foremost advocate of neoliberalism is the Foundation for Economic Freedom (FEF), whose honorary chair was Marcos's chief technocrat Cesar E.A. Virata.

3   The Multi-Fiber Agreement (MFA) granted favourable quotas to Philippine garment exports. This, however, expired in January 2005 upon the country's accession to the rules of the World Trade Organization.

Select Bibliography

Editorial

De Villers, Gauthier (2003), 'L'Etat en Afrique et la coopération internationale' in Totté Marc, Dahou Tarik et René Billaz (eds), *La décentralisation en Afrique de l'Ouest. Entre politique et développement*, Paris: Karthala.

Kama, Cissoko and Ramatou Touré (2005), 'Participation des acteurs sociaux et gouvernance d'Etat. Le cas du Cadre stratégique de lutte contre la pauvreté au Mali', *Politique Africaine* no. 99, October 2005.

Mounia Bennani-Chraïbi and Olivier Fillieule (eds) (2003), *Résistances et protestations dans les sociétés musulmanes*, Paris: Presses de Science Po.

Ould, Ahmed Salem Zekeria (1999), 'La démocratisation en Mauritanie', *Politique africaine*, October 1999.

Prasartset, Suthy (2004), 'From Victimized Communities to Movement Powers and Grassroots Democracy. The Case of the Assembly of the Poor' in Jayant Lele and Fahimul Quadir (eds), *Democracy and Civil Society in Asia*, Vol. 1: *Globalization, Democracy and Civil Society in Asia*, Palgrave Macmillan.

Raina, Vinod (ed.) (1997), *The Dispossessed. Victims of Development in Asia*, Hong Kong: Arena Press.

Stefanoni, Pablo and Hervé Do Alto (2006), *Evo Morales, de la coca al Palacio. Una oportunidad para la izquierda indígena*, La Paz: Editorial Malatesta.

Svampa, Maristella (2003), *Entre la ruta y el barrio. La experiencia de las organizaciones piqueteras*, Buenos Aires: Editorial Biblos.

Arab Peninsula

Al-Naqeeb, Khaldun (1990), *Society and State in the Gulf and Arab Peninsula*, London: Routledge.

Dazi-Héni, Fatiha (2006), *Monarchies et Sociétés. Le temps des confrontations*, Paris: Presses de Sciences Po.

Herb, M. (1991), *All in the Family: Absolutism, Evolution and Democratic Prospects in the Middle Eastern Monarchies*, Albany: State University of New York Press.

Salamé, Gh. (1991), 'Sur la causalité d'un manque: pourquoi le monde arabe n'est-il donc pas démocratique?' in *Revue française de Science Politique*, Vol. 41-3, June 1991, pp. 307–41.

Zahlan, R. S. (1998), *The Making of the Modern Gulf States*, London: Ithaca Press, 2nd edition.

Asia (general)

Boutros Gali, Boutros (1993), 'An Agenda for Democratizing' in Barry Holden, 2000, *Global Democracy: Key Debates,* London and New York.

Colas, Alejandro (2002), *International Civil Society*, Cambridge (UK): Polity Press.

Kongrut, Anchalee (2003), 'Creditor Comes Knocking: Japan Bank Wants Money Back at Once', *Bangkok Post*, 17 June.

Quizon, Antonio and Violeta Perez-Corral (1995), *The NGO Campaign on the Asian Development Bank,* Manila: Asian NGO Coalition for Agrarian Reform and Rural Development.

Indonesia

Khagram, Sanjeev (2000), 'Toward Democratic Governance for Sustainable Development: Transnational civil society organizing around big dams' in Ann M. Florini (ed.) *The Third Sector: The Rise of Transnational Civil Society*, Tokyo and Washington, DC: Japan Center for International Exchange & Carnegie Endowment for International Peace, pp. 83–114.

Leith, Denise (2003), *The Politics of Power: Freeport in Suharto's Indonesia*, Honolulu: University of Hawai'i Press.

Marut, Donatus K. (2003), 'Globalization and Conflicts among the Poor in Indonesia', Keynote and Column Speech in the Groenlinks [Greenleft] Party Conference, Groningen, Netherland, 25 October.

Kenya

Adar, G. K. (1998), 'Ethnicity and Ethnic Kings: The Enduring Dual Constraint in Kenya's Multi-ethnic Democratic Electoral Experiment', *Journal of Third World Spectrum*, Vol. 5, no. 2, 1998, pp.71–98.

Freeman, J. (1978), 'Crises and Conflicts in Social Movement Organization' in *Chrysalis: A Magazine of Women's Culture*, no. 5, 1978, pp. 43–51.

Freeman, J. (1999), 'On the Origins of Social Movements' in *Waves of Protest: Social Movements since the Sixties* (Rowman and Littlefield, 1999), pp. 7–24.

Heberle, R. (1951), *Social Movements: An Introduction to Political Sociology*, New York: Appleton.

Matanga, F. K. (2000), 'NGOs, the State and the Politics of Rural Development in Kenya with Specific Reference to Western Kenya', PhD Thesis, Rhodes University, Grahamstown.

Nairobi Law Monthly (Nairobi), August 1991; November 1991; December 1991.

Okumu, J. and Holmquist, F. (1984), 'Party and Party-State Relations' in J. D. Barkan (ed.), *Politics and Public Policy in Kenya and Tanzania*, New York: Praeger Publishers, pp. 45–69.

Republic of Kenya (1965), *Sessional Paper No. 10 on African Socialism and its Application to Kenya*, Nairobi: Government Printer.

Wikipedia, The Free Encyclopedia. Social Movements. http://en.wikipedia.org/ wiki/Social-movement.

Zirakzadeh, C. E. (1997), *Social Movements in Politics: A Comparative Study*, New York: Longman.

Philippines

Ariate, Joel F., Jr. (2005), 'Pork, Pigs, and Profit: State–Civil Society Relations in the Philippine Swine Industry in the Context of Globalization, 1995–2004' in Lopez Wui and Encarnacion Tadem, pp. 73–110.

Ariate, Joel F., Jr. (2005, 2006), 'More than Debt Relief: Two Decades of Freedom from Debt Coalition'. Research on 'Global Civil Society Movements: Dynamics in International Campaigns and National Implementation'. Sponsored by the Philippine Research Team–United Nations Research Institute for Social Development (PRT-UNRISD), pp. 1–26. Unpublished.

Bello, Walden, David Kinley and Elaine Elinson (1982), *Development Debacle: The World Bank in the Philippines*, California: Institute for Food and Development Policy.

Brillantes, Alex Jr. (1997), 'State–Civil Society Relations in Policy-making: Civil Society and the Executive' in Marlon A. Wui and Ma. Glenda S. Lopez Wui (eds), *State–Civil Society Relations in Policy-making*, 21–31. Quezon City: Third World Studies Center in Lopez Wui, Ma. Glenda S. and Teresa S. Encarnacion Tadem (eds), *People, Profit and Politics: State-Civil Society Relations in the Context of Globalization*, Quezon City: Third World Studies Center, University of the Philippines, Diliman. Published in cooperation with the United Nations Development Program (UNDP), Manila, pp. 19–71.

Lopez Wui, Ma. Glenda (2005), 'Engaging the State in the Context of Globalization: The Case of Civil Society Groups in the Garment Industry' in Lopez and Tadem (eds), *People, Profit and Politics: State-Civil Society Relations in the Context of Globalization*, Quezon City: Third World Studies Center, University of the Philippines, Diliman. Published in cooperation with the United Nations Development Program (UNDP), Manila, pp. 111–53.

Molmisa, Ronald (2005), 'State–Civil Society Interaction in a Liberalized Market: State–Civil Society Relations in the Telecommunications Industry' in Lopez Wui and Tadem (eds) (2005), *People, Profit and Politics: State-Civil Society Relations in the Context of Globalization*, Quezon City: Third World Studies Center, University of the Philippines, Diliman. Published in cooperation with the United Nations Development Program (UNDP), Manila, pp. 155–95.

Quinsaat, Sharon (2005), 'Mobilizing against Importation: State, Civil Society and the Benguet Vegetable Industry' in Lopez Wui and Tadem (eds), *People, Profit and Politics: State-Civil Society Relations in the Context of Globalization*, Quezon City: Third World Studies Center, University of the Philippines, Diliman. Published in cooperation with the United Nations Development Program (UNDP), Manila, pp. 19–71.

South Pacific

Bambridge, T. (2004), 'Mobilité et territorialité en Océanie', *L'information géographique* no. 68, pp. 195–211.

—— (forthcoming), *La terre dans l'archipel des îles Australes (Pacifique Sud)*, Editions de l'IRD-Aux Vent des Iles.

Belgrave, Michael, Kawharu Merata and David Williams (2005), *Waitangi Revisited: Perspectives on the Treaty of Waitangi*, Oxford: Oxford University Press.

Bonnemaison, J. (1985), 'The Tree and the Canoe: Roots and Mobility in Vanuatu Society', in Chapman M., *Mobility and Identity in the Pacific Islands*. Special edition of the Pacific Viewpoint, Wellington.

—— (1992), 'Le Territoire enchanté. Croyances et territorialités en Mélanésie', *Géographie et cultures*, no. 3, pp. 71–88.

Capeller, Wanda and Takanori Kitamura (1998), *Une introduction aux cultures juridiques non occidentales. Autour de Masaji Chiba*, Académie Européenne de Théorie du Droit de Bruxelles, Brussels: Editions Bruylant.

Chiba, Masaji (1993), 'Droit non-occidental' in André-Jean Arnaud, *Dictionnaire encyclopédique de théorie et de sociologie du droit*, Paris: LGDJ.

Clastres, Pierre (1974), *La Société contre l'Etat*, Paris: Les Editions de Minuit.

Cohen, Anthony P. (1994), *Self Consciousness: An Alternative Anthropology of Identity*, London: Routledge.

Crocombe, Ron (1992), 'The Future of Democracy in the Pacific Islands' in *Culture and Democracy in the South Pacific*, Institute of Pacific Studies. University of the South Pacific.

Firth, Raymond (1965), *Essays on Social Organization and Values*, London School of Economics. Monograph on social anthropology no. 28. Athlone Press.

Hau'ofa, Epeli (2000), 'The Ocean in Us' in A. Hooper (eds), *Culture and Sustainable Development in the Pacific*, Canberra: Asia Pacific Press, pp 32–43.

Hooper, Antony (ed.) (2000), *Culture and Sustainable Development in the Pacific*, Canberra: Asia Pacific Press.

Huffer E. and A. So'o (eds) (2000), *Governance in Samoa: Pulega i Samoa*, Canberra: Asia Pacific Press and Suva: Institute of Pacific Studies, University of the South Pacific.

Larmour, Peter (1997), *The Governance of Common Property in the Pacific Region*, Canberra, National Center for Development Studies, Research School of Pacific and Asian Studies, Australian National University. Series: Pacific Policy Papers No. 19, 223 .

Naepels, Michel (1998), *Histoires de terres Kanakes. Conflits et rapports sociaux dans la région de Houaïlou (Nouvelle-Calédonie)*, Paris: Editions Belin.

Ottino, Paul (1972), *Rangiroa: parenté étendue, résidence et terres dans un atoll polynésien*, Paris: Editions Cujas.

Régnault, J.-M. (2005), 'Une zone d'instabilité méconnue, le Pacifique insulaire', *Le Monde Diplomatique*, June 2005, p. 26-27.

—— (forthcoming), 'Vers la rupture des équilibres entre coutume, Etat, Eglise?' in *Relations Eglises et autorités outre-mer*, Paris: Les Indes Savantes.

Tui Atua Tupua Tamasese Taisi Tupuola Tufuga Efi (2004), 'Resident, Residence, Residency in Samoan Customs', *Symposium on Concepts in Polynesian Customary Law*, University of Waikato, New Zealand.

Sahlins, M. (2000), 'Identités et modernités du Pacifique', *La Nouvelle Revue du Pacifique*, Canberra: Australian National University, vol. 1, no. 1, pp. 19–25.

Wittersheim, E. (2006), *Des sociétés dans l'Etat. Anthropologie et situations postcoloniales en Mélanésie*, Editions Aux lieux d'être.

Turkey

Pasha, M. Kemal (2001), 'Globalization Islam and Resistance' in Gills, Barry K. (ed.) *Globalization and the Politics of Resistance*, New York: Palgrave.

Lelandais, Gülçin and Baris Baykan (2004), 'Cross-readings of the Anti-globalisation Movement in Turkey and Beyond. Political Culture in the Making', *International Social Science Journal*, No. 182, December.

Lelandais, Gülçin (2004), 'La société turque dans le défi de l'altermondialisation', *CEMOTI*, no. 37, January/July.

Index

Abhali Base Mjondolo, Durban shack dwellers movement, 139
Aborigines, 175
Abu Dhabi, Sheikh Khalifa, 91
activism, as profession, 189, 191
advocacy, 137-8; campaigns, 189
Afghanistan, US aggression against, 73-4
Africa: external consumption democracy, 2; networks against the debt, 9
African National Congress (ANC), South Africa, 141-2
African Social Forums (ASF); Bamako 2002, 146; Conkary 2005, 111
African Union, 128; Commission, 111
Agricultural Sector Alliance of the Philippines, 195
agriculture: debts, 156; farmer suicides, 5, 157;free trade agreements impact, 21, 62, 147; job losses, 40; small-scale farmer displacement, 178; US subsidized, 40, 52
Ahmadinejad, Mahmoud, rhetoric of, 101
aid, as censorship, 190
Al Ahma, Sabah, 91
Al Maktûm, Muhammad Bin Râshid, 90
Al Nahya clans, 91
Al Naqeeb, Khaldun, 88
Al Saoud dynasty, Saudi Arabia, 91
All-Ceylon Fisheries Trade Union, 184
alliances: making of, 195; popular movements, 42
'Andean-Amazonian capitalism', proposal for, 32
Anti-NGO club, Thailand, 162
Anti-Privatization Forum, South Africa, 139, 141
anti-war movement, Turkey, 106
Arab world: alternative discourse, 69; Arabization question, 82; democracy advocates, 68
Arab Peninsula, economic austerity period, 87; new social pacts, 89
Argentina, 2, 56-7; Cromagnon 'massacre', 49; unemployed (*piqueteros*) movement, 8, 46-7, 51; -Uruguay conflict, 59
aristocratic principles, Oceania, 173
armed conflict, Colombia prolonged, 61

armed forces, Mexico, 55
Asian Development Bank: actions against, 103, 154-5; annual conference 2000, 153; Asian networks against, 9
Asian NGO Coalition on Agrarian Reform and Rural Development, 154
Assembly of the Poor, Thailand, 8, 161-2
Association of Muslim Jurists, Thailand, 164
Australia, 174; 'Oceania policeman', 175
authoritarianism, 88, 115, 132; dictatorships declining power, 2
autonomous political expression, Algerian lack of, 79

Bahrain, 89
Bakrie, Aburizal, 186-7
Bamako, Mali: ASF 2002, 146; Polycentric Social Forum, 111
Bank for Information Center, Washington, 154
Barak, Ehoud, 98
Barcelona process, 93
basic necessities: price rise struggles, 94, 120, 140, 142; subsidies removal, 5; VAT added, 119
Battle, Jorge, 57
Bayelsa state, Nigeria, 132
Bemba, Jean-Pierre, 129
Benedict XVI, 188
Benin, 2, 111
Berberism, 82; cultural movement (MCB), 84
Bhopal, victims, 158
Bishop, Christopher, 124
Black Friday 1983, Venezuela, 36
Blair, Tony, 109
Bolivarian Revolution, Venezuela, 35, 38
Bolivia, 56, 138; anti-privatization mobilizations, 58; collective action laboratory, 29; ethnically discriminatory foundation, 30; national capitalism periods, 33; social movements, 55
Bomas draft constitution, Kenya, 116
Bono, 109
Bosch, Mariette, 124
Botswana Democratic Party, 124-5